PRAISE FOR
GOALS-BASED INVESTING

Tony Davidow has effectively captured the evolution of modern wealth management by focusing on the key determinants of financial success. This gem is a must-read for both financial advisors and individual investors.

—**John Nersesian,** CIMA®, CFP, CPWA®, Head of Advisor Education, PIMCO Investments

With this book, Tony Davidow strikes the perfect balance of explaining success in wealth management as both an "art" and a "science." He carefully threads the needle with advice, anecdotes, and wisdom that will inspire financial advisors everywhere.

—**April Rudin,** Founder and CEO, Rudin Group

I have known Tony Davidow professionally for 20-plus years and know him to be a thought leader on the topics of goals-based investing, alternative investments, ESG, and behavioral finance. I think this book is an essential reference source for any advisor who wants to better understand the current and future states of wealth management for high-net-worth families.

—**Scott Welch,** CIMA®, Board Member of the Investments & Wealth Institute

I am seeing a growing number of institutional investors evolve their portfolios, moving assets into foreign markets, seeking to enhance the yield in their fixed-income portfolio, and increasing allocations to alternative investments, such as private equity, real assets, and hedge funds. As high-net-worth investors and their advisors seek to upgrade their portfolios and emulate the success of institutional investors, *Goals-Based Investing* provides the rationale and road map to facilitate the journey.

—**Keith Black,** PhD, CFA, CAIA, FDP Managing Director, Content Strategy, CAIA Association

True leaders do way more than just effectively lead—they educate, they motivate, and they lay a strong foundation for others to succeed in their footsteps. In the decade plus that I've personally experienced the leadership of Tony Davidow, he has embraced every one of these traits of leadership in the financial advisory universe. His new book is a fantastic, concise blueprint for how advisors need to evolve—a must-read for every A-list advisor.

> —**Kevin Sánchez,** CIMA®, CPWA®, CFP, former Chair,
> Investments & Wealth Institute

The wealth management industry is undergoing a secular shift from product to advice. In this context, Tony Davidow captures the evolution of the advisor/client dialogue as it has moved beyond "the money" to a host of noninvestment needs. *Goals-Based Investing* is equally useful for investors who are often confused by their choices of products and advisors and for advisors who need to deliver much more than investment returns to meet their clients' idiosyncratic objectives.

> —**Jamie McLaughlin,** CEO, J. H. McLaughlin & Co., LLC

With each passing year, client expectations rise. Those that are not on a learning journey will find themselves left behind. Tony Davidow is a consummate teacher and well-equipped Sherpa who contextualizes the changing world of wealth management and provides pointed guidance to help advisors better serve high-net-worth clients.

> —**Christine Gaze,** Founder and Managing Partner,
> Purpose Consulting Group

After decades as an advisor to financial advisors and experience in working with institutional money managers and funds, Tony is sharing his knowledge and insights in long-term wealth management. *Goals-Based Investing* is a timely book for financial advisors wanting to succeed and address their client's needs in the current market environment. Additionally, do-it-yourself investors would benefit from reading *Goals-Based Investing,* with up-to-date information on market developments, techniques for asset allocation, and wealth management.

> —**Halvard Kvaale,** Portfolio Manager, former Head of Manager
> Research & Due Diligence, National Broker-Dealer

In his book *Goals-Based Investing,* Tony Davidow fuses the diverse landscape of investing into one succinct and comprehensive treatment to help investors navigate the world of wealth management. Whether you are a financial advisor or DIY investor, you will find relevant insights to help build and manage portfolios. From behavioral finance to alternative assets, to sustainable investing and more, Davidow covers it all.

—**Margaret M. Towle,** PhD, CIMA®, CPWA®, Yakima River Partners, LLC

Goals-Based Investing is a must-read for fiduciaries and advisors. Tony Davidow uncovers financial myths, discloses the market realities, and everything in between. Tony takes us on a journey exploring the evolution of the wealth management industry.

—**Alan Reid,** Founder and CEO, rPartners

Tony Davidow was my original teacher and mentor on all things investing as I was coming up in financial services. He taught by showing, not just telling. He does not talk down to the retail investor. Yet he manages to help them meaningfully elevate their understanding of investing and leverage its benefits to help meet their goals.

—**Lule Demmissie,** President, Ally Invest

GOALS-BASED
INVESTING

A VISIONARY FRAMEWORK FOR WEALTH MANAGEMENT

TONY DAVIDOW, CIMA®

New York   Chicago   San Francisco   Athens   London   Madrid
Mexico City   Milan   New Delhi   Singapore   Sydney   Toronto

1 2 3 4 5 6 7 8 9   LCR   26 25 24 23 22 21

ISBN   978-1-264-26820-7
MHID   1-264-26820-3

e-ISBN   978-1-264-26821-4
e-MHID   1-264-26821-1

This publication is designed to provide accurate and authoritative information in regard to the subject matter covered. It is sold with the understanding that neither the author nor the publisher is engaged in rendering legal, accounting, securities trading, or other professional services. If legal advice or other expert assistance is required, the services of a competent professional person should be sought.

—From a Declaration of Principles Jointly Adopted by a Committee of the American Bar Association and a Committee of Publishers and Associations

Library of Congress Cataloging-in-Publication Data

Names: Davidow, Tony, author.
Title: Goals-based investing : a visionary framework for wealth management / Tony Davidow, CIMA.
Description: New York : McGraw Hill, [2022] | Includes bibliographical references and index.
Identifiers: LCCN 2021021210 (print) | LCCN 2021021211 (ebook) | ISBN 9781264268207 (hardback) | ISBN 9781264268214 (ebook)
Subjects: LCSH: Portfolio management. | Investments.
Classification: LCC HG4529.5 .D375 2021 (print) | LCC HG4529.5 (ebook) | DDC 332.6—dc23
LC record available at https://lccn.loc.gov/2021021210
LC ebook record available at https://lccn.loc.gov/2021021211

Contents

Acknowledgments

I HAVE WANTED TO WRITE A BOOK FOR MANY YEARS, BUT DUE TO company restrictions and time commitments, I was never able to start the journey. I have written dozens of white papers, blogs, and articles addressing some of the topics and themes covered in this book, and I have spoken at hundreds of conferences over the past couple of decades addressing the changing wealth management landscape. I have read hundreds of books on the history of Wall Street, investment strategy, behavioral finance, and modern portfolio theory, but I felt there was a void: a book written specifically for wealth advisors, providing guidance on evolving their practices, value proposition, and investment acumen. This book is also written for the high-net-worth investor who has largely been making their own investment decisions.

In writing my first book, I was fortunate to have a team of people help me through the process. My Advisory Board encouraged me to write a book because they thought I had something of value to share. They reviewed chapters, offered constructive feedback, and wrote reviews. I owe a debt of gratitude to John Nersesian, Margaret Towle, Alan Reid, Scott Welch, Jamie McLaughlin, Christine Gaze, Bob Powell, and Halvard Kvaale for their guidance and friendship.

My early views on investing and dealing with wealthy families were impacted by Hans Jepson and Charlie Schulman. They took a chance on a young farm boy with no investing experience. Hans and Charlie taught me many valuable lessons that have led to my writing this book, and I am fortunate to count them both as friends and mentors after these many years.

I have been honored to be involved in the Investments & Wealth Institute in various capacities for over 25 years, serving on the Board of Directors, chairing multiple committees (National Conference, Government Relations, and Nominating Committee), and currently serving as chair of the Editorial Advisory Board of the *Investments & Wealth Monitor*. The organization provides certification programs, advanced education, and cutting-edge thought leadership. It marries academic rigor delivered by Ivy League professors and practical application delivered by strategists and industry experts.

The conferences and publications have helped shape my views and perspective. Many of the staff and the volunteers have become friends. Sean Walters, CEO, wrote the foreword to my book; Devin Ekberg, chief learning officer, and Debbie Nochlin, editorial director, helped in editing and promoting my book. I would like to thank the Editorial Advisory Board for identifying the challenges and opportunities facing the industry. You helped shape the changing landscape addressed in this book.

I would like to thank Kevin Sanchez, April Rudin, Keith Black, Lule Demmissie, Joe Burns, and Tatiana Esipovich for reading my manuscript and providing feedback. I have been fortunate to work with many of the top wealth managers across the industry, including Alex Williams, Peter Rukeyser, Rob Sechan, Jim Schlueter, Mike Appleton, Ivar Bolander, Brian Ullsperger, Dorothy Bossung, Todd Wagenberg, and Noel Paccaro-Brown. You elevate the profession through your dedication and investment in yourselves and your practices. My industry friends have supported me throughout the years, including Liz Ann Sonders, Laura McDowell, Garry Bridgeman, Betsy Piper-Bach, Libet Anderson, Jonathan Golub, Bob Worthington, Bruce Stewart, Donal Mastrangelo, Becky Bowler, Jeaneen Terrio, Pete Sloan, Brett Wright, Joel Schiffman, Luke Collins, David Archer, and Peter Gorman.

When I discussed writing a book, I was told that I needed an agent, perhaps the best advice that I received. My agent, Leah Spiro, has been my guiding light through this maiden voyage. She believed in me from the beginning and provided wise counsel throughout the process. Leah helped me present my manuscript to the top publishers in the industry and helped me evaluate the offers I received to publish this book.

I selected McGraw Hill largely because of Stephen Isaacs. Stephen liked my early manuscript and knew the audience that I was targeting. He has impressive credentials, working with many of the top authors in the investment industry, but remained approachable and accessible throughout this process. His team, including Judith Newlin, Scott Sewell, Steve Straus, and many others, have been helpful and professional in all aspects of editing, publishing, and marketing *Goals-Based Investing: A Visionary Framework for Wealth Management*.

I would like to thank Natalia Cervantes, who has been crucial in marketing and promoting my book. Natalia has helped me in building my website, social media presence, and overall awareness about my book. She has been passionate about the project, and her expertise has helped reach an ever-growing audience.

Last, I would like to thank my loving wife, Sovy, and our two talented daughters, Stephanie and Megan. They are all passionate teachers, helping educate the next generation and prepare them for this ever-evolving world. I know that they will make a difference in the next generation and instill a curiosity that will serve them well. Our family has always been focused on making a difference and educating others.

Putting the words on paper took a couple of months, but my experiences and perspective come from several decades, often spending weeks on the road meeting with clients and speaking at conferences. There were too many missed birthdays, anniversaries, and special events. My family always understood that was part of my job and that I was trying to help advisors and investors achieve better outcomes. I have been fortunate to have a loving family and strong support system.

Foreword

I FIRST MET TONY AT AN INVESTMENT CONSULTING CONFERENCE we were holding in New York. He was enthusiastically explaining his "laddering" approach to professional development for Morgan Stanley advisors. In the credentialing world today, his approach to educating advisors would be defined as "stackable." His ideas would be considered on the cusp today, let alone 15 years ago when I met this friendly, generous executive from one of the leading advisory firms in the business.

When I was asked to pen a foreword to a new book from one of our most prolific and thoughtful subject matter experts among our community of volunteers, I was quite honored. I have served as CEO of the not-for-profit Investments & Wealth Institute since 2010. The Investments & Wealth Institute is a professional association representing the brightest advisors in the world discussing the most pressing issues of the day, backed by academic research.

The notion of setting the proverbial table for as broad and comprehensive a work as *Goals-Based Investing: A Visionary Framework for Wealth Management*, however, is a bit intimidating. The book examines topics to which our organization has devoted whole courses, conferences, publications, and research. I've been fortunate to eavesdrop on a decade of conversations about the very topics presented in this book: the evolution and future of wealth management, active versus passive investing, alternative investing, private markets, sustainable investing, and goals-based investing. Tony Davidow has been a nucleus anchoring the center of so many of these conversations for more than 25 years. Tony has taught in our Certified Investment Management Analyst certification program, delivered dozens of educational sessions and webinars, and served for many years as editor of our award-winning, peer-reviewed publication, the *Investments & Wealth Monitor*. In 2020, he was recipient of our prestigious J. Richard Joyner Wealth Management Impact award, presented to individuals who have contributed exceptional advancements in the field of private wealth management.

This book's release is timely. The modern financial advisor profession is less than a half century old. The financial planning movement began formally in 1969, with the creation of the International Association for Financial Planning (now the Financial Planning Association, College for Financial Planning, and Certified Financial Planner Board of Standards). The investment consulting movement began formally in 1985 with the creation of the Investment Management Consultants Association (now the Investments & Wealth Institute). These two movements have benefited the public in tremendous ways, establishing a rising bar of professionalism for financial advisors and transforming the industry that employs or serves financial advisors.

For several years our institute has conducted research on clients who work with an advisor, in an effort to understand what differentiates exceptional advisors from good advisors. This research tells us that foundational expectations of clients are that their advisors are committed to ethics, that they help them achieve their goals, and that they place clients' needs above other, competing interests. Beyond that, they expect expertise, a personalized approach, advanced capabilities, exceptional service, and meaningful guidance.

These differentiating characteristics are indeed the very substance and character of this book, and have been at the heart of the body of work over which Tony has labored for many years. Tony was ahead of the curve 15 years ago when we met, and he still sees more clearly than most that the wealth management profession is transforming at a rapid pace because of many factors: Regulation, competition from new business models, and advances in technology are driving the way advisors do business and changing advice delivery to meet client expectations.

The good news is that the future of wealth management can be navigated with the right skills and competencies. Advisors will continue to succeed by evolving in tandem with the investment and wealth management industry. This book tackles the endeavor of arming today's practitioner with the knowledge to be more successful, and addresses key trends toward which successful advisors have either begun transitioning their practice or have already found success in following.

I applaud Tony Davidow for the timely arrival of *Goals-Based Investing: A Visionary Framework for Wealth Management*, offering us practical, innovative solutions for delivering wealth management services and financial advice, based on the solid foundation of globally applicable investment management principles. The reader is in for a treat!

Sean R. Walters, Chief Executive Officer, Investments & Wealth Institute

Introduction

THE FINANCIAL SERVICES INDUSTRY IS AT A KEY INFLECTION POINT. Wall Street firms are under scrutiny due to built-in conflicts of interest, and robots threaten to replace financial advisors. Financial advisors are trying to remain relevant and valued by investors, and their fees are coming under pressure. Many are evolving to become wealth advisors, which requires an expanded set of capabilities. A plethora of new products have come to the markets, and advisors and investors need help using them effectively. The industry has experienced a rapid transformation over the past decade. *Goals-Based Investing: A Visionary Framework for Wealth Management* examines the implications of this transformation.

In the current market environment, wealth advisors need to evolve their approach to investing to better serve their clients. *Goals-Based Investing* provides a framework for addressing client needs. Wealth advisors need to expand their number of asset classes to identify investment opportunities and to adequately diversify risk in the portfolios they manage. Modern portfolio theory is no longer modern and even postmodern portfolio theory is passé. The financial markets are more interconnected than they have ever been before: what happens in China affects the global markets, as do issues such as geopolitical risks, demographic shifts, technological advances, and social tensions around the world.

Fortunately, investing products have evolved significantly over the past few decades, which makes it easier for advisors and investors to access various market segments and unique asset classes such as hedge funds, private equity, private credit, and real assets. Exchange-traded funds (ETFs), registered funds, and feeder funds have helped democratize investing. *Goals-Based Investing* considers some of the structural trade-offs of new products coming to the market and examines how wealth advisors can effectively incorporate these new tools when building and managing client portfolios. Wealth advisors need to evolve their practices and value proposition to keep pace with the rapidly evolving industry. Otherwise, they risk becoming commoditized and left behind.

RESPONDING TO THESE CHALLENGES

I have been researching, writing, training, and speaking to tens of thousands of advisors over the years on such diverse topics as working with high-net-worth (HNW) investors, advanced asset allocation, factor investing, and the role and use of alternative investments. For most of my 35-year career, including stints at Schwab, Guggenheim Investments, Morgan Stanley, and Kidder Peabody, among others, I have led with education, so both advisors and investors are better informed. I have worked directly with hundreds of HNW and ultra-high-net-worth (UHNW) families in developing and implementing asset allocation strategies, and I have worked closely with large institutions and family offices to provide a range of consulting services. In fact, I began my career working for a large family office and gained invaluable experience that has served me well throughout my career.

Throughout my career, I have sought out those wiser than I and often challenged conventional wisdom, whether it pertains to investment theory or how to engage clients. Many mentors have shaped the way I view the world. In turn, I have mentored many young professionals on their journeys. I have been fortunate to meet many Nobel laureates over the years, including Harry Markowitz, Bill Sharpe, Eugene Fama, Robert Merton, Richard Thaler, Daniel Kahneman, and Myron Scholes. I have been in awe of their genius and thankful for their contributions as the industry has evolved from academic theory to practical implementation.

I have worked with thousands of advisors who have a variety of professional certifications, including CIMA® (Certified Investment Management Analysts), CPWA® (Certified Private Wealth Advisors), RMA® (Retirement Management Advisors), CFA® (Chartered Financial Analysts), and CAIA® (Chartered Alternative Investment Analysts). These sophisticated advisors are the primary audience for *Goals-Based Investing*, with a specific focus on advisors who work with HNW investors ($1 million to $20 million in investable assets) and UHNW investors ($20 million or more in investable assets). Financial advisors serving HNW and UHNW investors understand the need for advanced education to adequately serve their clients' needs. I view this segment of financial advisors as "lifelong learners": constantly seeking to learn and invest in themselves. They recognize that nothing remains the same, and those who do not evolve risk becoming obsolete.

This book also addresses the challenges faced by family offices, multifamily offices (MFOs), and sophisticated HNW investors, who leverage multiple experts in an unbundled fashion. Family offices and MFOs often employ investment and tax professionals and are focused on sourcing unique investment opportunities (private equity, private real estate, private credit, and hedge funds, among others), that can be integrated and accessed across multiple accounts (personal, trusts, family foundation, etc.). Family office and MFO professionals have multiple relationships across a variety of firms, from traditional investment management to private equity and tax planning. Family offices often have one or more foundations to fund charitable activities and may have dedicated personnel to manage the foundation.

This book also provides insights that can be leveraged by sophisticated HNW investors, many of whom have worked in the financial services industry or have sold their companies and perhaps have a core competency in a particular segment of the market, but are looking to diversify outside of their area of expertise. Many of my friends work or have worked for wealth management firms, asset managers, hedge funds, private equity, and real estate firms. They may not need help in their area of expertise, but would benefit from unbundled advice to augment their areas of expertise. They may not use a financial advisor in the traditional sense, based on their experience, and may employ multiple experts to source ideas and investments.

HNW and UHNW investors are focused on meeting their family's goals, transferring wealth to future generations, funding charitable endeavors, and setting up trusts to protect their wealth, among other issues. They likely invest in hedge funds, private equity, private credit, and real assets, among other complex investments. HNW families may have an affinity for socially responsible investing, aligning their portfolios and purposes. *Goals Based Investing* is designed to provide a framework for addressing family needs in an ever-evolving environment. To bring some of these concepts to life, I incorporate personal experiences and case studies throughout the book.

CHAPTER 1

The State of the Financial Services Industry

Holding onto a sound policy through thick and thin is both extraordinarily difficult and extraordinarily important work. This is why investors can benefit from developing and sticking with sound investment policies and practices. The cost of infidelity to your own commitments can be very high.

Charles D. Ellis
Winning the Loser's Game: Timeless Strategies for Successful Investing

THE FINANCIAL SERVICES INDUSTRY IS AT A CRITICAL TURNING point. To succeed in this new landscape, financial advisors need to understand how the environment has changed and how they must evolve their approach. This chapter provides the backdrop for the rest of the book by introducing the challenges facing the industry broadly and financial advisors specifically. Advisors who embrace these changes and lean into them are more likely to be successful than advisors who resist change and keep trying to work with clients by following an increasingly out-of-date playbook.

For investors, it is often confusing to understand the nomenclature and the roles that each party plays. Before we delve into the state of the industry, let's identify the key players and their various roles.

TABLE 1.1 **The Key Players in Wealth Management**

Player	Other Names Used to Describe Firms	Examples	Roles
Wealth management firms	Full-service firms (wirehouses), registered investment advisor (RIA), and independent broker-dealers	Morgan Stanley, Merrill Lynch, Goldman Sachs, UBS, Raymond James, LPL, and Hightower	Provide research, due diligence, and operational support to financial advisors. Provide scale and efficiency to support financial advisors who work with clients.
Financial advisors	Financial consultant, wealth advisor, and investment consultant	Financial advisors work for wealth management firms.	Provide advice on a range of issues to clients. May employ asset managers to provide investment advice.
Custodians	N/A	Schwab, Fidelity, Pershing	Provide custodial services, technology, research, and trading support to RIAs.
Asset managers	Investment manager, and money manager	Blackrock, PIMCO, Fidelity, Vanguard, JP Morgan, American Century, Nuveen, etc.	Manage money via various structures, including mutual funds, separately managed accounts (SMAs), exchange-traded funds (ETFs), and hedge funds.

Several firms play multiple roles, which can add to investor confusion. Morgan Stanley, UBS, and Goldman Sachs are wealth management firms with both retail and private wealth divisions (>$10 million in investable assets), as well as asset management subsidiaries. JP Morgan is a bank with retail, private wealth, and asset management businesses. Schwab and Fidelity are custodians with retail and asset management businesses. Blackrock and PIMCO are asset managers that provide investment solutions to retail, HNW, and institutional investors, including separately managed accounts (SMAs), mutual funds, exchange-traded funds (ETFs), and alternative investment strategies.

Several trends have transformed the industry over the past couple of decades. The changes have affected the firms, the business models, and the various players' relationships.

FEE COMPRESSION AND ALIGNMENT OF INTEREST

One challenge facing the industry is the increasing pressure on the fees that financial advisors charge clients. The public is much more skeptical about the financial advice that advisors provide. More and more, clients are asking their advisors, "Are you serving *me?* Or are you serving *yourself?*" There is also confusion about what a client is paying for and whether it represents a fair value.

In the 1980s, financial advisors received most of their compensation in the form of commissions. They were compensated for recommending individual stocks, bonds, mutual funds, and annuities. Their incentive was to generate a lot of activity to increase their commissions. In fact, the wealth management firms would often establish goals regarding how much commission they needed to generate per product. Financial advisors who generated a lot of commissions were rewarded with incentive trips, higher payouts, and officer titles (vice president, senior vice president, executive director, managing director, etc.).

In the early 1990s, the industry began to embrace another compensation structure that better aligned the advisor's activities and the client's interest. Rather than relying solely on commissions, many financial advisors began adopting some form of advisory model, in which their compensation was based on their client's assets under management. This structure better aligned the advisor and client, because the advisor was now incented to increase the assets under management. The advisor shared in the client's successes: more assets meant higher fees for the advisor.

While this was a step in the right direction for the industry, clients saw an ability to generate market-beating results as the advisor's value proposition. The advisory fee structure only considered the client's investment portfolio. The client often did not pay a fee directly for financial planning work, retirement planning, estate planning, holding unmanaged assets, and general counseling services, even though these services provided significant value.

In the client's mind, the value of the advisor was too often equated with the ability to beat the market. Through the roaring bull market of the 1990s, advisors could tout how well their client's portfolios had grown and how their compensation had risen dramatically as well. Advisors embraced the notion that their value proposition was accessing world-class investment managers and growing their clients' assets under management. Financial advisors could charge a premium fee on top of the manager's fees, because the investment results were strong as the markets soared to new highs.

The 2000s ushered in a new environment, with the bursting of the dot-com bubble (2000) and the global financial crisis (GFC; 2008). Many clients gravitated toward strategies offering the highest returns, so they paid a big price when the dot-com bubble burst and tech-heavy strategies lost significant value. Many advisors deflected accountability by blaming investment managers, who were easily replaced.

After the dot-com bubble, many advisors fell back into the trap of recommending high-flying managers to clients. These were not the tech-laden growth managers who dominated the late 1990s. Instead, value managers who espoused the values and virtues of Warren Buffet became the new darlings. They claimed that their disciplined approach would keep investors away from another debacle like the dot-com bubble. These managers claimed insights and skills in identifying undervalued companies and avoiding the blowups.

Financial advisors also began encouraging investors to allocate assets to international and emerging markets. These markets offered diversification benefits and helped insulate investors from events affecting the US markets. The international and emerging markets managers boasted of their ability to identify the next Microsoft, Apple, or Google. It was a very compelling story, and the data showed strong investment returns outside US borders in the early 2000s.

As Figure 1.1 illustrates, emerging markets was the best-performing asset class in 2003–2007, and 2009. Therefore, it is not surprising that many advisors were recommending emerging markets managers to their clients heading into the GFC of 2008. Of course, the GFC affected virtually all market segments, pushing the S&P 500 down 37 percent, international markets down 43 percent, and emerging markets down a staggering 53 percent.

Many investors felt shell-shocked after the dot-com bubble and GFC. They began to question the value of having an advisor. *Can my advisor really outperform the market? Do advisors have access to the best investment managers? Are our interests truly aligned?*

We have seen a great deal of fee compression over the past couple of years. This has been fueled in part by lower-cost solutions, an increasingly competitive landscape, and a lack of appreciation of advisor value. Investors often feel that the advice they receive is cookie-cutter and is therefore a commodity.

Many advisors have embraced ETFs as building blocks, but this does not lessen the value of the financial advisor. In fact, it demonstrates that advisors are focused on providing low-cost market exposure. An advisor's value is in assembling the appropriate underlying investments that provide the highest likelihood of achieving client goals. To do that effectively, financial advisors must consider cost, tax efficiency, and performance in a product-agnostic fashion. Financial advisors may need to recast the way they describe their services to clients, but they should not feel compelled to discount their fees merely because they are using cheaper solutions.

FIGURE 1.1 Select Asset Class Returns (2000–2009)

2000	2001	2002	2003	2004	2005	2006	2007	2008	2009
Core Bonds 11.6%	Core Bonds 8.4%	Core Bonds 10.3%	EM 56.3%	EM 25.6%	EM 34.5%	EM 32.6%	EM 39.8%	Core Bonds 5.2%	EM 78.5%
T-bills 6.0%	T-bills 4.1%	T-bills 1.7%	US Sm Cap 47.3%	Int'l Dev 20.1%	Int'l Dev 14.0%	Int'l Dev 26.9%	Int'l Dev 11.6%	T-bills 1.8%	High-Yield Bonds 63.5%
High-Yield Bonds −2.0%	US Sm Cap 2.5%	EM −6.0%	Int'l Dev 39.2%	US Sm Cap 18.3%	US Lg Cap 4.9%	US Sm Cap 18.4%	Core Bonds 7.0%	High-Yield Bonds −28.4%	Int'l Dev 31.8%
US Sm Cap −3.0%	High-Yield Bonds −1.1%	High-Yield Bonds −10.0%	High-Yield Bonds 34.1%	High-Yield Bonds 11.3%	US Sm Cap 4.5%	US Lg Cap 15.8%	US Lg Cap 5.5%	US Sm Cap −33.8%	US Sm Cap 27.2%
US Lg Cap −9.1%	EM −2.4%	Int'l Dev −15.7%	US Lg Cap 28.7%	US Lg Cap 10.9%	High-Yield Bonds 3.1%	High-Yield Bonds 12.0%	T-bills 4.7%	US Lg Cap −37.0%	US Lg Cap 26.5%
Int'l Dev −14.0%	US Lg Cap −11.9%	US Sm Cap −20.5%	Core Bonds 4.1%	Core Bonds 4.3%	T-bills 3.0%	T-bills 4.5%	High-Yield Bonds 2.1%	Int'l Dev −43.4%	Core Bonds 5.9%
EM −30.6%	Int'l Dev −21.2%	US Lg Cap −22.1%	T-bills 1.1%	T-bills 1.2%	Core Bonds 2.4%	Core Bonds 4.3%	US Sm Cap −1.6%	EM −53.3%	T-bills 0.2%

Source: Morningstar Direct

Clients who don't perceive any value from having an advisor assemble portfolios may choose to build their own portfolios using ETFs. In fact, in rising bull markets investors often think they do not need any help investing. That was the case in the late 1990s and in our most recent bull run. Clients typically remember the value of advice when market volatility rears its ugly head.

With increased competition for HNW investors, the industry has seen steady fee compression over the past decade. Wealth management firms squeeze mutual fund and SMA managers to reduce their fees, and financial advisors undercut their competitors to gain market share. Lower fees are good for investors, but may also mean that wealth management firms and asset managers may be forced to eliminate client service support, training programs, and due diligence personnel charged with finding and vetting new managers and strategies. Asset managers may need to eliminate staff who support advisors and create materials for clients. Managers may also choose to not participate in advisory programs that pay reduced fees.

THE RISE OF PASSIVE INVESTING

Jack Bogle, founder of The Vanguard Group, created the first index fund in 1975. Bogle believed that low-cost index funds were better for investors than high-cost mutual funds that attempt to outperform the market. At the time, he did not receive a lot of credit. Today, Vanguard is the second-largest asset manager in the world, with more than $6 trillion in assets under management. Bogle has also spawned a group of rabid followers, known as "Bogleheads." His investing philosophy goes like this:

1. Select low-cost funds.
2. Carefully consider the added costs of advice.
3. Do not overrate past fund performance.
4. Use past performance to determine consistency and risk.
5. Beware of star mutual fund managers.

6. Beware of asset size.
7. Do not own too many funds.
8. Buy your fund and hold it.

Bogle was cynical about the value of a financial advisor. He felt that investors did not need the additional cost of advice and would do just as well on their own. Vanguard softened this anti-advisor rhetoric in later years, as it wanted advisors to embrace Vanguard mutual funds and ETFs, but Bogle planted the seed that investors could choose to invest for themselves.

Although the first ETF was introduced in 1993, ETF growth really accelerated after the GFC. Investors questioned why they should pay such high fees if investment managers were unable to protect them from market collapses or even outperform the market during its collapse. Many advisors began to use ETFs to build diversified portfolios. They could efficiently access markets at substantially lower fees than either mutual funds or SMAs. They quickly pivoted their value proposition to assembling port-folios with an expanded set of cost-effective and tax-efficient strategies.

Today, there are more than $5 trillion in ETF assets under man-agement. While the top four firms (Blackrock, Vanguard, State Street, and Invesco) represent roughly 80 percent of the industry's assets under management, many of the traditional asset managers have joined the party, as they have seen outflows from their mutual fund and SMA businesses. Firms like JP Morgan, Goldman Sachs, PIMCO, Nuveen, Fidelity, and Franklin have entered this growing marketplace.

The growth of ETFs also corresponds to the rapid rise of Rep-as-PM and Rep-as-Advisor programs across Wall Street. These advisory programs let financial advisors collect a fee for building portfolios in either a discretionary or nondiscretionary fashion. Advisors could use stocks, bonds, mutual funds, and ETFs to gain exposure to market segments. ETFs were the perfect tool for these programs, with their ease of trading and ability to access virtually all markets. Unified managed accounts also used ETFs, attracted by their low cost, tax efficiency, and ease of access.

THE DISRUPTORS

Though Jack Bogle is credited with starting the passive indexing craze, Charles Schwab introduced several innovations that have helped transform the financial services industry. He founded Charles Schwab in 1975 as a discount broker, challenging the high commissions Wall Street firms charged. Schwab later introduced the first Mutual Fund Marketplace, as well as no-transaction-fee mutual fund and ETF platforms. The firm also launched a robo-asset allocation program and a robo-financial-planning program, ushering in the era of digital advice. In the fall of 2019, the firm introduced zero commissions on equities, ETFs, and options. Schwab has focused on helping the individual investor by breaking down barriers and increasing access.

Schwab has also emerged as the largest custodian for the burgeoning independent registered investment advisor (RIA) market. In 2020, Schwab completed the acquisition of TD Ameritrade, increasing its market share of the growing RIA business.

Chuck Schwab and Jack Bogle are credited with disrupting the financial services industry, but they are not alone. Betterment and Wealthfront started the robo-craze and were quickly followed by Schwab, Vanguard, and Fidelity, among others. Even the large established full-service firms have offered some form of digital advice. Firms like SoFi and Robinhood have also jumped into the fray, offering so-called free trading to millennials and smaller investors.

All this disruption has served to further bifurcate the marketplace, with retail investors often getting digital advice and cookie-cutter solutions, and HNW investors demanding highly customized, integrated advice. This is confusing, because many of the firms claim to provide similar services. If investors can't distinguish between advice quality, they will likely opt for the low-cost solution.

ASSET MANAGEMENT TRANSFORMATION

Asset managers have had to respond to the changing landscape as well. Their fees for mutual funds and SMAs have been reduced, and they have had to combat the rise of low-cost, passive investing strategies. Many asset managers have decided to launch ETFs to counter the outflows of their active strategies, or acquire ETF providers to jump-start their entry into the fast-growing ETF marketplace.

Based on the challenges in outperforming passive benchmarks, active equity managers have seen net outflows since 2008 (see Figure 1.2). According to the 2020 ICI Fact Book, equity assets under management fell to $11.3 trillion as of December 2019. Conversely, ETFs grew dramatically over the same period, with domestic assets now topping $5 trillion. I am not suggesting that mutual funds will become obsolete, but recognizing the seismic shift underway as investors embrace ETFs.

Many asset managers have decided to offset the outflow of mutual fund assets by entering the ETF marketplace, so they have to deal with the reality of dramatically lower margins. This shift affects their ability to support wealth management firms and financial advisors, both monetarily and through sales and marketing support. Most asset managers pay to be included on platforms (wirehouses and custodians). Asset managers often pay some form of revenue sharing to include their mutual funds, SMAs, and ETFs on the various platforms. Larger asset managers may be asked to become a partner firm, which means paying a substantial fee for preferential treatment: internal sales data, product placement, and access to advisors.

Fee compression brings several unintended consequences. Asset managers may choose to hold back capacity-constrained strategies from platforms, and smaller asset managers may choose to not participate in platforms. Ultimately, financial advisors and investors pay the price in the form of limited investment options.

Many asset managers have sought to improve their revenues by either offering higher-margin products such as alternative

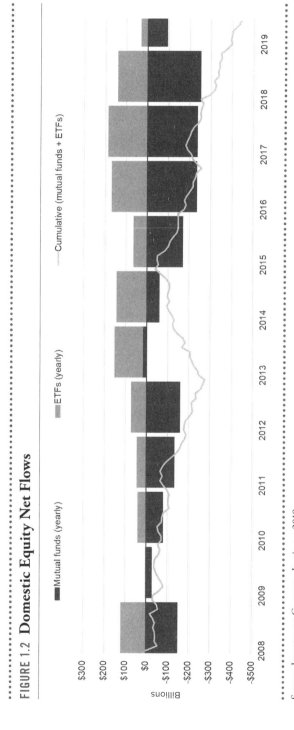

FIGURE 1.2 Domestic Equity Net Flows

Mutual funds (yearly) ETFs (yearly) Cumulative (mutual funds + ETFs)

Billions

$300 $200 $100 $0 -$100 -$200 -$300 -$400 -$500

2008 2009 2010 2011 2012 2013 2014 2015 2016 2017 2018 2019

Source: Investment Company Institute, 2019

11

investments (hedge funds, private equity, private credit, and real assets) or solutions that capture more assets (model portfolios). To broaden their product offerings, asset managers either developed these capabilities, partnered with experts, or acquired firms with the expertise.

ALTERNATIVE INVESTMENTS: HEDGE FUNDS

After the dot-com bubble, HNW investors began demanding access to alternative investments and other unique strategies. HNW investors wanted efficient ways to protect themselves from market corrections and wanted exposure to the best investments. They wanted access to hedge funds.

Hedge fund growth exploded in the late 1990s when top traders at Goldman Sachs, Morgan Stanley, and others left to set up their own firms. Hedge funds let managers make a lot of money without the restrictions of large firms' compliance and oversight. Hedge fund managers could charge a hefty management fee, typically 2 percent, plus a performance fee of 20 percent (often referred to as "2 & 20"), and sometimes even more. Hedge funds had limited capacity and were only available to institutions and wealthy families (qualified purchasers or accredited investors).

The Securities and Exchange Commission (SEC) uses the term *accredited investors* to indicate investors who are financially sophisticated and have less need for the protection provided by regulatory disclosure filings. Accredited investors include HNW investors, banks, insurance companies, brokers, and trusts. To be an accredited investor, an HNW investor must have an annual salary of $200,000 or greater for the past two years, or a net worth of $1 million, excluding their home's value.

As demand grew, many Wall Street firms began to offer their HNW investors access to hedge funds. Because of the limited capacity, and the merits of diversification, funds of funds (FoFs) became a popular choice for many of these firms. FoFs offered diversification across multiple underlying hedge funds, spreading the risks across managers and strategies. FoF managers would tout their due diligence expertise and access to otherwise unavailable hedge funds. Unfortunately, FoFs carry an additional layering of fees, on top of the hedge funds' already high prices. That is quite a burden to overcome.

After the GFC, many investors were disappointed that hedge funds lost money, albeit not as much as most traditional investments. Many of these hedge funds were promising absolute returns regardless of market conditions, capturing some incremental returns quarter over quarter in rising and falling markets. Also, several large FoFs had been allocating capital to Bernie Madoff. (Madoff technically was not running a hedge fund, but rather an elaborate Ponzi scheme.)

Investors yet again questioned the merits of these strategies. *Is there proper alignment with hedge fund fees? Are the fees excessive? Is absolute return just a marketing gimmick? How come my FoF did not identify Madoff's fraud through their due diligence?*

LIQUID ALTERNATIVES

Liquid alternative investments—hedge fund strategies in a mutual fund structure—became popular after the GFC. Asset managers were quick to jump into the fray whether they had experience managing hedge fund strategies or not. Liquid alternatives addressed some of the structural challenges with hedge funds: excessive fees, lack of liquidity, and lack of transparency. Liquid alternatives were also available at lower minimums. Retail investors could select from a plethora of new products. Liquid alternatives' assets under management grew rapidly after the GFC, but have slowed significantly in recent years.

Although there are advantages to offering alternative investments in a more liquid and transparent structure, there are also trade-offs in providing liquidity.

TABLE 1.2 **Pros and Cons of Liquid Alternatives**

Pros	Cons
Offered in a liquid, transparent, and regulated structure	Certain strategies do not fit in a liquid structure.
Available to all investors—no accredited investor requirements	Liquid alternatives may need to retain cash to meet redemptions.
Limited use of leverage and derivatives	Limited use of leverage may limit return potential.
Frequent pricing and valuations	Pricing depends on the underlying investments.
Tax reporting: 1099 versus K-1	Performance may lag because of constraints.

In recent years, some investors have criticized the performance of liquid alternative strategies. There are a few reasons for this criticism, some valid and some not:

- **Mismatch in expectations.** Investors expected alternatives to outperform in a rising bull market.
- **Cash drag.** Holding cash or liquid securities to meet redemptions served as a drag on returns.
- **Manager experience.** Many managers lack experience in managing long/short strategies.
- **Economics.** Managers may have an incentive to include their best ideas in the limited partnership (LP) structure rather than in their mutual fund surrogates, because of the favorable economics.

Liquid alternatives sound appealing on the surface, but we need to explore some of the structural trade-offs. Liquidity comes at a price. The best managers may limit their best ideas to large investors that are not as likely to seek redemptions and pay higher fees. An increasing number of liquid alternative closures have occurred over the past couple of years. We will continue to evaluate these results in the coming years.

I will cover alternative investments in greater detail later in this book, but I will point out now that demand from HNW investors and recognition from many top-tier hedge funds and private equity funds has led to further product evolution. Registered funds have become an attractive hybrid solution that addresses some of the structural concerns of the classic LP structure and the limitations of liquid alternatives. The number and quality of the products coming to the market has improved dramatically in the past several years.

PRACTICE EVOLUTION

Financial advisors serving HNW investors are often called wealth advisors—a term that better reflects the work they do for their clients—but which also forced these advisors to reinvent themselves and provide new and different services for their clients. That reinvention requires new skills and education. Advisors need a better understanding of trust and estate issues, concentrated positions, lending options, and charitable giving, among other issues. Financial advisors often formed teams to tackle these areas.

To meet the needs of HNW investors, advisors may need advanced education on a broader set of investment options, including ETFs, factor investing, alternative investments, and private markets. Advisors need to understand the merits of these strategies and their structures including open-end funds, closed-end funds, hedge funds, feeder funds, interval funds, and auction funds, to name a few.

Many of the large wealth management firms have developed internal training programs to educate their advisors about the needs of HNW investors, as well as programs geared to improving financial advisors' investment acumen. Many financial advisors have taken education programs from industry organizations such as the Investments & Wealth Institute, CFA Institute, CAIA Association, and Financial Planning Association (FPA), among others. Investments & Wealth Institute introduced the Certified Investment

Management Analyst (CIMA) program in the early 1990s, because advisors were seeking education beyond what their firms could offer. The Investments & Wealth Institute later introduced the Certified Private Wealth Advisor (CPWA) program to hone the skills of advisors serving HNW investors, and the Retirement Management Analyst (RMA) program to help advisors serving retirees. The CFA Institute offers the CFA certificate for members who pass a comprehensive program designed to help advisors in portfolio management. CAIA introduced the CAIA Charter to provide advanced education regarding the role and use of alternative investments. The FPA administers the Certified Financial Planning (CFP) designation.

TABLE 1.3 Industry Certifications

CIMA	CPWA	CFA	CFP	CAIA
Investment Consulting	Private Wealth Management	Portfolio Management	Financial Planning	Alternative Investments
• Fundamentals of investing • Investment theory • Behavioral finance • Risk management • Portfolio construction • Consulting process • Ethics	• Advanced tax • Estate planning • Charitable giving • Complex issues: business owners and executives • Retirement planning • Family wealth dynamics • Ethics	• Quantitative methods • Corporate finance • Financial reporting and analysis • Portfolio management • Investments • Ethics	• Intro to financial planning • Insurance planning • Investments • Fundamental tax • Retirement planning • Estate planning • Ethics	• Private markets • Hedge funds and managed futures • Real assets • Structured products • Asset allocation • Risk management • Due diligence
≈9,000 certificants	≈2,500 certificants	170,000 certificants	>88,000 certificants	>11,000 certificants

Totals as of January 2021.

These advanced designations help financial advisors distinguish themselves in a crowded marketplace. Many advisors also attain multiple advanced designations to fulfill their intellectual curiosity.

These lifelong learners are motivated to remain the best at their profession.

PRACTICE DIVERSITY

Advisors should carefully consider their teams' diversity. The financial services industry has long been dominated by older white men. As an industry, we need to do a much better job in attracting women, minorities, and younger professionals. Teams benefit from diverse perspectives, and investors want to engage with people who are more like them.

Table 1.4 shows the demographic breakdown of women, African American, Asian, and Hispanic financial advisors. Women represent more than half of the US population, but make up a mere 32.1 percent of the advisor population. That's substantially more than the percentage of African American, Asian, and Hispanic advisors (6.9 percent, 8.6 percent, and 6.3 percent, respectively).

TABLE 1.4 **Percentage of Women and Minority Advisors**

Member Group	Percent of Advisor Population
White	82.2%
Women	32.1%
Black	6.9%
Asian	8.6%
Hispanic	6.3%

Source: Bureau of Labor Statistics, 2019

Several organizations, such as the Investments & Wealth Institute, have developed formal initiatives to address diversity and inclusion. Wealth management firms such as Morgan Stanley and RBC have developed their own diversity initiatives and mentoring programs to change the complexion of the financial services industry.

Women represent a substantial growth opportunity. As McKinsey predicts, "An unprecedented amount of assets will shift into the hands of U.S. women over the next three to five years, representing a $30 trillion opportunity by the end of the decade."[1] Attracting and retaining women investors will be of critical importance. Financial advisors need to include spouses and children in fostering relationships with HNW families. They need to think about the transfer of wealth to the next generation.

Tiger Woods had a profound impact on the game of golf, not just because of his otherworldly talents, but perhaps more important, because he broke the stereotype that golfers are a bunch of rich white men. Woods inspired kids with his athletic prowess and the fact that he looked different from other golfers: his father was African American and his mother was Asian. A generation of male and female golfers have grown up idolizing Tiger Woods. Minority children saw someone who looked like them succeed and were inspired by his amazing accomplishments.

As an industry, we need to show minorities that there is a path for them to be successful in the wealth management industry. We need to celebrate those who have achieved success and foster an inclusive environment so that others will follow their lead. Wealth management firms and asset managers should offer better training programs for minorities and recruit them out of college. This is good for the industry and good for individual practices that strive to serve a diverse clientele.

As Table 1.5 illustrates, millennials are the largest population cohort and the largest portion of the workforce. Millennials largely grew up during a period of economic and technological expansion; 9/11 and the GFC helped shape them. Told by parents, teachers, and coaches that they were special and entitled, they are confident and self-assured. This generation was burdened by college debt and few job opportunities after graduation. These experiences shaped their philosophy and approach.

Millennials are a growing opportunity, based on their sheer size and the way they make decisions. They look to peers for guidance and validation. They get information from social media, shop online, and are typically tech-savvy. Millennials have embraced robo-advice and online trading platforms such as Robinhood. Successful financial advisors will need to bring on younger advisors to reach this growing segment and must embrace the way they engage millennials by leveraging technology.

TABLE 1.5 **Generation Breakdown**

Generation	Birth Years	Population Billions (%)	Labor Force Billions (%)
Millennial	1981–1996	72.5 (22.0%)	59.4 (31.6%)
Gen X	1965–1980	62.5 (19.8%)	53.4 (28.3%)
Boomer	1946–1964	72.0 (21.8%)	36.1 (19.2%)

Source: Pew Research Center, US Census Bureau

THRIVING IN A POST-COVID WORLD

The world stopped when the COVID-19 pandemic hit in 2020. Investors worried about their health and whether they would have enough money to weather the storm.

Beyond the health issues, investors sought guidance about the markets and their portfolios. Financial advisors needed to pivot quickly from a robust economy to an economy intentionally put to sleep to save lives. They had to deal with unprecedented market volatility and uncertainty about when the markets would stabilize. The precipitous declines in February and March were very troubling for investors, and no doubt many considered heading for the exits to avoid further losses. Investors heard daily death tolls, saw ravaging images, and watched their wealth plummet.

Table 1.6 shows that 8 of the 10 largest point losses of the Dow Jones Industrial Average (DJIA) occurred in 2020; 8 of the 10 largest point gains also occurred in 2020. Only 2 of the 10 largest percentage losses occurred in 2020. Because the markets were at all-time highs, the point losses and gains exaggerate the overall percentage moves from lower levels. By comparison, the largest percentage loss occurred on Black Monday, October 19, 1987, when the Dow fell a then-record 508 points (–22.61%).

TABLE 1.6 **Largest Point Losses of the DJIA**

Rank	Date	Point Loss	% Loss
1	March 16, 2020	–2,997.10	–12.93
2	March 12, 2020	–2,352.60	–9.99
3	March 9, 2020	–2,013.76	–7.79
4	June 11, 2020	–1,861.82	–6.90
5	March 11, 2020	–1,464.94	–5.86
6	March 18, 2020	–1,338.46	–6.30
7	February 27, 2020	–1,190.95	–4.42
8	February 5, 2020	–1,172.29	–4.60
9	February 8, 2018	–1,032.89	–4.15
10	February 24, 2020	–1,031.61	–3.56

During the pandemic, financial advisors needed to help their clients with both their finances and their emotions. In many respects, COVID-19 accelerated some of the trends already underway. Financial advisors had to reimagine ways to engage clients, such as using technology to reach clients and provide practice efficiency. They needed to hone their behavioral coaching skills and investment acumen to provide sound advice during this tumultuous period. Advisors needed to probe their clients' needs beyond the portfolio. Did they need additional income? How were they feeling about market volatility? How often should they reach out to each client? What should they review?

As of the writing of this book, we are still dealing with the effects of COVID-19 and learning how to engage clients. We have gotten accustomed to Zoom calls, social distancing, and working remotely. Financial advisors consume information by reading research, listening to webinars, and attending virtual conferences.

It is not clear how advisors will engage clients in a postpandemic world: in person, remotely, through technology, or some combination of each. This potentially changes the business model in serving existing clients and bringing in new clients. Financial advisors need to reexamine their practice size and functional responsibilities—they need to reevaluate their value proposition—and may need to reinvent themselves as wealth advisors.

Many financial advisors have not fully made that transition to wealth advisors. If they do not evolve their approach, they risk becoming commoditized or worse, obsolete. Financial advisors need to recognize the changes and challenges identified in this chapter and continue to evolve the way they serve their clients. If they do not, they risk being replaced by robots or seeing their practices shrink over time.

CHAPTER 2

The Evolution of Wealth Management

The best way to measure your investing success is not by whether you're beating the market, but by whether you've put in place a financial plan and a behavioral discipline that are likely to get you where you want to go.

Benjamin Graham

THE WEALTH MANAGEMENT INDUSTRY IS AT A KEY INFLECTION point and is undergoing a transformation. Wealth management firms and financial advisors are evolving their business models to effectively serve HNW investors. They are also moving away from a primarily transaction-oriented model to a relationship-oriented model. Financial advisors have had to invest in themselves and recast their value proposition to remain a relevant and vital part of their clients' universe. They have had to expand their investment knowledge beyond traditional investments and broaden the set of services they provide to a more discerning clientele.

Wealth management is much more than managing money. It is a multidisciplinary approach to solving the needs and desires of wealthy families. Investment management is the means to the end.

It can fund families' activities, such as passing on wealth from one generation to the next or charitable giving. Investment management can generate income through retirement or to fund the purchase of a home.

Advisors often tout their investment management expertise as their core value proposition. They highlight their success in outperforming the market by picking mutual funds or SMAs that have historically outperformed. Not surprisingly, investors often gauge their advisors' success or failure based solely on performance. If their advisors fail to outpace the market, they seek others who promise that they will.

Advisors need to change the way they are valued and evaluated. Outperforming the market often comes from taking aggressive shortsighted bets, rather than developing a long-term strategic plan and making subtle adjustments as appropriate. An advisor's value to clients is much more than outperforming the market.

Investors have become skeptical about conflicts of interest and concerned about the level of fees they pay. They are often confused by industry jargon and are unable to distinguish between the capabilities that various wealth management firms offer. Investors and clients struggle to properly *value* their relationships.

This chapter covers the transformation underway and discusses how advisors need to respond to the changing landscape. It reviews the needs and expectations of HNW investors and how advisors can stand out and flourish, rather than become commoditized. This is a journey that requires a big investment of time and money—but one that will pay big dividends in the future.

THE EVOLUTION TO A WEALTH ADVISOR

The role of advisors has evolved considerably over the past several decades, as shown in Figure 2.1.

FIGURE 2.1 The Evolution to a Wealth Advisor

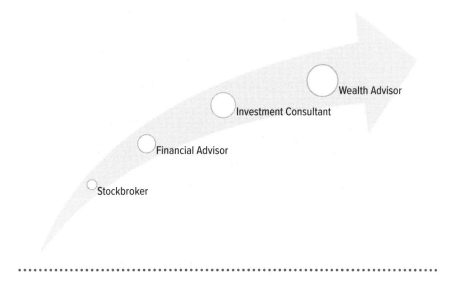

From Stockbroker to Financial Advisor

This first stage of evolution occurred several decades ago, so this brief description should be familiar to most readers. Advisors evolved from stockbrokers, who pitched stocks touted by their firms, to financial advisors, who promoted an array of financial products, including mutual funds, SMAs, insurance products, and initial public offerings (IPOs). Financial advisors often were incented to sell a proprietary product recommended by the firm. Based on how much they sold, advisors got higher payouts and recognition, including trips, from the firms employing them.

From Financial Advisor to Investment Consultant

As the industry evolved, many firms created a different business model, to better align advisors and investors. Investment consultants adopted a process like those employed by institutional consultants to understand each client's goals and objectives, develop an investment policy statement and asset allocation strategy, conduct manager searches, and monitor underlying manager performance. Consultants often adjusted the process to incorporate reviews of trusts and estates, plus other unique issues for HNW investors.

FIGURE 2.2 **The Consulting Process**

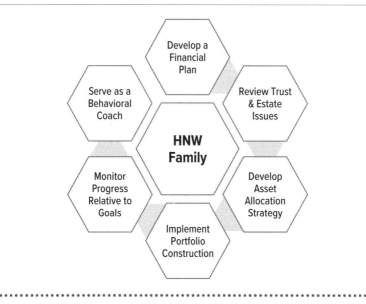

The evolution of the investment consultant coincided with the introduction of consulting businesses across Wall Street. These businesses conducted due diligence and identified institutional-quality investment managers. The businesses negotiated favorable pricing and made them available to advisors via a wrap-fee structure. These third-party managers managed SMAs and mutual funds.

The consulting businesses developed tools and training to help convert advisors to this new model. Advisors migrated to this model because it aligned advisor and investor interests by changing advisor compensation from commissions to advisory fees. The advisor charged a fee based on assets under management (AUM), and fees rose and fell based on portfolio value.

These businesses grew dramatically across the industry as advisors and investors gravitated to this new model. Advisors liked the idea of open architecture and the recurring revenue model. They got paid quarterly and could leverage third-party managers to grow their businesses.

Investors gained access to world-class managers and liked the aligned economic model. They appreciated that advisors were helping them achieve their goals and were not motivated by generating commissions. Investors could see their portfolios grow and felt comforted that they had a team of experts managing their money.

Let's take a closer look at each step in the consulting process.

Develop a financial plan. Consultants assess clients' needs and objectives. Consultants elicit information about their clients' experience, risk appetite, return expectations, time horizon, and cash-flow needs. This information goes into a financial plan that serves as a client road map.

Review trust and estate issues. Consultants should understand all pertinent information around clients' trust and estate issues, charitable giving goals, and large concentrated positions. Consultants may want to discuss gifting strategies for low-basis securities and consider setting up multiple trusts.

Develop an asset allocation strategy. Consultants should develop a long-term strategic allocation that provides a high likelihood of achieving clients' goals and objectives. The allocations should consider a range of asset classes that have historically exhibited attractive return, risk, and correlation characteristics. Consultants may need to develop multiple asset allocations across the various account types (personal, retirement, trusts, family foundations, etc.).

Implement portfolio construction. Whereas asset allocation provides a theoretical framework for dividing capital among a range of asset classes, portfolio construction is how an investor gains exposure to the underlying asset classes. Consultants may use individual securities, mutual funds, SMAs, ETFs, or alternative investments to gain exposure to these asset classes. Consultants must properly integrate asset allocation and portfolio construction to achieve clients' goals and objectives.

Monitor progress relative to goals. Once the consultant has developed an asset allocation and portfolio construction strategy, he or she establishes the frequency and means to measure progress relative to each client's goals. Benchmarking has some inherent limitations. For example, performance relative to the S&P 500 or some other benchmark (60% S&P 500 / 40% Barclays Aggregate) may or may not be relevant to some clients.

Become a behavioral coach. Perhaps a consultant's greatest value is in serving as a behavioral coach to help clients make rational decisions and avoid emotional responses. Consultants should understand what their clients mean—not only what they say—and help their clients through behavioral biases that we all know exist. A behavioral coach keeps clients engaged when things feel the most uncomfortable.

From Investment Consultant to Wealth Advisor

As advisors began to pursue larger clients, they recognized the need to expand their skills beyond merely offering traditional money management. Many of the larger Wall Street firms developed internal training programs to enhance advisors' skill sets. Advisors who successfully completed these programs often earned designations such as "wealth advisor." (Different firms may use slightly different titles.)

Industry groups such as the Investments & Wealth Institute developed the CIMA program to hone investment consulting skills and the CPWA to help advisors who focus on HNW and UHNW families. These programs leveraged academics and brought in industry experts to discuss such topics as asset allocation, alternative investments, tax planning, estate planning, charitable giving, executive compensation, and dealing with concentrated positions. These certifications helped advisors distinguish themselves from their competitors. They demonstrated to clients (both current and potential) that an advisor had attained an advanced level of education, knowledge, and skills about managing investments for HNW and UHNW clients.

HOW THIS ADVISOR EVOLUTION HAS IMPACTED WEALTH MANAGEMENT FIRMS

As wealth management firms evolved their business models, they wanted their advisors to move their practices upstream to serve larger families with more complex needs. They recognized that the competition for smaller accounts was growing and that smaller accounts offered fewer opportunities to add significant value. The HNW market represented a target-rich opportunity, with significant wealth being created and transferred from one generation to the next.

According to the Capgemini 2020 *World Wealth Report*,[1] there are approximately 5.9 million HNW investors in America: investors with $1 million or more in investable assets. There are 120,000 UHNW investors: investors with $30 million* or more in investable assets. As more firms target larger clients, some have segmented their businesses and invested in training their advisors to effectively handle the complexities of wealth. The training and tiering have been geared toward educating advisors about the unique challenges and issues wealthy families face. Advisors learned advanced wealth management techniques and often were able to leverage firm resources for wealthy families.

---

* Capgemini uses $30 million as a minimum for this group; however, most wealth management firms use $20 million as the entry point.

As an industry, we have seen a big shift to team-based models. Team members often have a diverse set of skills. Teaming gives advisor practices scale, efficiency, and expertise. A team structure also reassures clients that their wealth advisor has bench strength, diverse skill sets, and backup coverage.

Figure 2.3 illustrates how the financial services industry has become segmented. Though the industry may be segmented and there are significant differences between the coverage model and related experience, these differences are not always clear to investors. Advisors must distinguish themselves when targeting wealthy families. Many may earn advance certifications, such as the CIMA, CPWA, CAIA, RMA, and CFP. Advisors should highlight team members' capabilities and experience, as well as any accreditations they've earned.

FIGURE 2.3 Segmenting the Financial Services Industry

UHNW investor is generally defined as >$20 million in investable assets, and HNW investor is defined as $1 million–$20 million. Mass Affluent investors have between $100,000–$1 million.

Private Wealth Management

Morgan Stanley, Goldman Sachs, Merrill Lynch, UBS, and JP Morgan have dedicated teams focused on serving the needs of UHNW families. These businesses are often called "private wealth management" or "private client groups." They are typically structured in teams and usually handle only 30 to 50 families. Some of these teams are focused on certain industries and may be aligned with investment banking coverage.

These teams handle fewer families in part so they can develop deep relationships with their clients. Private wealth teams often work with founders and senior executives of private companies. They often cultivate relationships before an IPO; the connections typically flourish once a company goes public. These teams often have trust and estate experts who work with founders in establishing trusts and funding activities before a company goes public. They have specialists who can assist in establishing preset diversification programs (PDP) for corporate insiders. Teams have access to unique investment opportunities, including IPOs, hedge funds, private equity, private debt, and private real estate.

Global Wealth Management

Global wealth management firms (also known as wirehouses)— Morgan Stanley, Merrill Lynch, UBS, and Wells Fargo—have teams focused on HNW and mass-affluent investors, as well as institutions, retirees, business owners, and other client segments. They typically leverage firm resources to handle challenging issues. The teams focused on HNW investors are often required to complete internal training and sometimes advanced industry training. These teams typically handle several hundred clients, some of whom receive preferential treatment.

The industry is becoming more bifurcated. HNW investors demand highly customized advice. Smaller investors opt for non-human interactions and may be reluctant to pay advisory fees, because they often see little value. Advisors must focus on investors who value advice and need help in meeting their objectives. HNW investors with complex circumstances—including taxes, trusts, concentrated positions, charitable giving, and multiple entities—need a skilled advisor to help navigate them through myriad challenges and issues.

Wirehouses also handle mass-affluent clients and have been moving smaller clients toward some form of digital advice offering (also known as "robo-advice"). Advisors handling mass-affluent clients typically have several hundred clients and are encourage to cross-sell product to improve client retention and increase revenue.

A small cadre of advisors focus on dealing with institutional clients. They often have advanced education in types of institutions (pension plans, public funds, endowments and foundations, etc.) and their needs, and frequently have teams and resources dedicated to institutional customers.

Retail/Digital Services

Charles Schwab, Fidelity, and Vanguard have been aggressive in launching robo-asset allocation and robo-financial planning tools to their retail clients. The robo-offerings provide scale and efficiency. Without human intervention, however, it is not clear that investors will remain disciplined through challenging periods. After all, we are only human, and we are tempted to let fear and euphoria take the reins in extreme situations. Robinhood offers a trading platform targeting millennials, but little advice in valuing securities, understanding financial markets, or building portfolios.

Registered Investment Advisors (RIAs)

Schwab, Fidelity, and Pershing provide custodial services to registered investment advisors (RIAs) who serve clients across the wealth spectrum (retail, HNW, and UNHW). The RIA segment has grown dramatically over the last several years, fueled by large advisory teams leaving the wirehouses. The growth of the RIA model has been fueled by the advisor's desire for independence and the public's perception of Wall Street. As industry veteran Charlotte Beyer noted:

> Today, financial services as a whole still suffer from an erosion of trust. The 2008–09 financial crisis strained relationships; the tension between a client's sense of entitlement and the advisor's need to scale for profitability was like a fragile power line in a snowstorm. The history of our industry is littered with scandals like Bernie Madoff and Wall Street's own focus on short-term profits, destroying good faith in an entire industry.[2]

Beyer was criticizing large firms' focus on generating profits from clients, rather than serving their needs. After the GFC, many investors began to question larger firms' built-in conflicts of interest: the use of affiliated products, revenue sharing with asset managers, and investment banking conflicts, among others.

The RIA segment has seen strong growth following the GFC, as advisors wanted to distance themselves from their Wall Street roots. They wanted to avoid looking like they were out to make money *from* clients and focus their practices on making money *for* clients.

The RIAs tout their independence and ability to serve as a fiduciary to their clients: to put the client's interests first. Generally, wirehouse advisors are held to a lesser standard and often cannot acknowledge that they are a fiduciary. RIAs can develop their own investment philosophies, conduct independent due diligence, and use tools and technology they choose. This market segment will continue to grow in the years to come.

Though wirehouses are hesitant to universally acknowledge that their advisors may be fiduciaries, many of the advisors are fiduciaries and conduct themselves accordingly. I have spent the vast majority of my career working directly with advisors, and most are honorable, putting client interests first. In fact, many of the accreditation organizations have codes of conduct (ethical standards) mandating that their members act in their client's best interests.

PUTTING THEORY INTO PRACTICE

HNW and UHNW families have multiple issues to contend with. Wealth advisors should consider cash-flow needs and estate-planning issues before developing an asset allocation strategy. They should evaluate the tax consequences and asset locations, and may need to determine how to fund charitable activities. These issues are interrelated.

FIGURE 2.4 **Wealth Management Issues of High-Net-Worth and Ultra-High-Net-Worth Families**

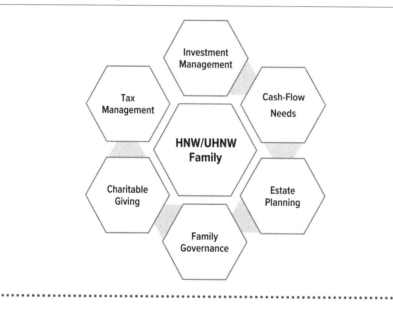

In the late 1990s to mid-2000s, I worked in Morgan Stanley's Private Wealth Management division, managing Graystone Wealth Management and serving as a member of the Client Strategy Group. Morgan Stanley acquired Graystone, a multifamily office with particular expertise in alternative investments, to bolster its Private Wealth Management division's investment offering to UHNW families.

The Client Strategy Group was an elite group of professionals deployed to work with the firm's largest clients and prospects, who were often selling a business or going public via an IPO. The Client Strategy Group had team members with expertise in trust and estate issues, executive compensation, hedging and monetization strategies, and tax management. I was the resident expert on asset allocation and alternative investments. We worked closely on all large complex situations, which was a competitive advantage.

The Client Strategy Group was often brought in to work with the founder or senior executives of a company before or after an IPO. Before the IPO, our trust and estate team discussed setting up trusts, titling assets, and potential gifting strategies. Because many corporate executives are restricted in their ability to sell securities, our team discussed hedging and monetization strategies, including setting up a PDP, which establishes a plan for insiders to sell securities at predetermined intervals and amounts. These programs helped corporate executives gain liquidity and diversify their holdings, without running afoul of insider trading rules.

Taxes are a major consideration for any wealthy family going through an IPO or business sale. Ideally, tax planning should occur before the transaction to minimize the tax impact, which can be substantial. Advisors must deal with several critical issues up front, including:

- How should assets be titled?
- Has the family set up trusts for children or grandchildren? What kind of trusts?
- How should taxes be paid? Which entity should pay them?
- Should you gift securities before selling a company or IPO?
- How can we minimize taxes? How should we allocate sale proceeds?

Developing an asset allocation strategy has some unique complexities as well. Founders and senior executives typically have the lion's share of their wealth in their company stock. Financial theory would suggest diversifying the concentrated position. However, restrictions may mean that this isn't feasible, or the optics and emotional attachments might make it unpalatable. Founders are often hesitant to sell shares because selling might suggest that they have lost confidence in the company. They often feel an emotional attachment to the stock, because it created their wealth.

An asset allocation strategy for a founder or senior executive may need to be implemented over an extended period of time, as securities are liquidated. Diversifying exposure by avoiding certain industries or market sectors, to minimize risk concentration, may be prudent. For example, a technology company founder might avoid additional technology exposure. Different accounts—personal investments, trusts for children or grandchildren, a family foundation—will probably require different asset allocations.

Because many founders tie up their wealth in restricted stock and options, they may be asset rich, but liquidity constrained. A cash-management program can help them handle taxes and other expenditures.

This section talks about the challenges facing UHNW families and the need for specialized resources to help them respond appropriately. Although there are many similarities in the issues UHNW families face, every family is unique in the way it responds to these issues.

A TEAM OF EXPERTS

Because of the varied issues affecting HNW and UHNW families, they may employ multiple advisors to assist in specialized areas, such as investment management, executive compensation, estate planning, and tax management. Family offices may bring in resources to handle these issues and help define family legacy and governance issues. Family offices typically take care of investment, tax, and philanthropic needs for families with $250 million or more in investable assets. Multifamily offices handle the needs of multiple families, providing scale, expertise, and efficiencies.

Regardless of how they handle these areas, advisors shouldn't view these issues in isolation. Teams need coordination and integration. Advisors may also need to leverage internal and external expertise around the various issues. They may need to work with other trusted advisors engaged by the family, including trust and estate attorneys, tax advisors, and corporate council.

Many wealth advisors have formed teams to help address the issues facing HNW families, with internal and external experts. Teams may include former trust and estate attorneys; they may be able to leverage firm resources designated for the wealthiest clients. They will need investment management expertise, often with in-depth knowledge of hedge funds, private markets (private equity, private credit, and real assets), and other complex products. Some teams will establish relationships with local experts to broaden their expertise and reach. These relationships may also be a source of referral business.

For example, a UHNW family that just sold its business for $100 million wants a dedicated team that is familiar with company sales and establishing PDP programs. The family wants an expert to review trust documents and may want advice on setting up additional trusts. The family will want to leverage expertise in considering potential gifting strategies and properly titling of assets. Senior executives will want guidance regarding executive compensation, including restricted stock and option grants. Depending on the nature of the sale and the underlying liquidity, the family may need to consider lending options.

Last, when the family is ready to develop an investment plan, they want someone who can develop an asset allocation strategy across multiple account types. The family will expect access to unique investment options, including hedge funds, private equity, private real estate, and other nontraditional investments, and clarity around tax implications.

In summary, UHNW families want a dedicated team, with related experience and sufficient resources to serve their needs. Private wealth teams typically handle only UHNW clients, have deep teams and resources, and handle only 40 to 50 families. Their average client relationship may be $40 million to $50 million and they provide a high-touch approach to handling a family's needs.

Conversely, wirehouse teams typically handle hundreds of HNW families and leverage firm resources, and their average client often ranges from $1 million to $5 million. This is not to suggest that the wirehouse team isn't capable of handling a $100 million family—but it is not their norm, and they may not have experience in dealing with the issues facing the family.

DEVELOPING A WEALTH MANAGEMENT PROCESS

As discussed, advisors are focusing on moving their practices upstream, serving wealthier families with more complex needs. They are developing specialized teams and trying to right-size their practices so they can properly support client needs. It's challenging for teams to learn all the essential information about a particular family if they have several hundred clients. Some advisors systematically transition smaller relationships to junior team members or other advisors. For some advisors, this has been a natural evolution. Others have struggled to reinvent themselves.

To properly scale their practices and adequately meet client expectations, teams need to develop a wealth management process that captures all relevant information about a family's goals. They may have various goals for different accounts. A family may focus on wealth preservation for personal assets and wealth accumulation for children's trust accounts. The family might establish specific funding goals for a family foundation and could want to maintain an opportunistic trading account.

Teams must elicit information from the family and guide them through the decision-making process, considering:

- What are the family's goals and objectives? The family may have multiple objectives.
- What is the client's overarching investing philosophy?

- What are the key considerations: taxes, intergenerational transfer of wealth, legacy planning, and so on?
- What cash-flow needs does the family have?
- How should the family measure success?
- What is the family's mission statement?
- What are their philanthropic needs?
- How often should the advisor revisit the family's goals?

The goal is to become a trusted advisor: someone with whom the family feels comfortable discussing wealth, taxes, legacy planning, family dynamics, and other sensitive topics. It often takes time to earn a family's trust. Over time, the family may feel more comfortable sharing additional information; therefore, advisors should continue to engage clients and keep abreast of any changes to their circumstances. Families make changes; marriages, divorces, births, selling businesses, purchasing homes, and replacing attorneys, CPAs, and financial advisors all happen. Advisors who don't pay attention may find that someone else will, and they may be at risk of losing clients.

Capgemini notes that HNW investors are scrutinizing the size and nature of their advisory fees. "More than one in five HNWIs might switch firms in the next year, with high fees being the top reason for 42% of HNWIs. HNWIs are also citing a preference for performance and service-based fees over asset-based ones, indicating higher expectations on value delivered for fees charged."[3]

As an industry, advisors need to address fee structure. As mentioned at the beginning of this chapter, advisors moved from earning commissions to receiving a percentage of assets under management. This advisory model better aligns advisor and client interests; by aligning the fees with performance, it reinforces the advisor's relationship with the portfolio. This model ignores the value provided in working through issues around trusts and estates, charitable giving, family legacy, and large concentrated positions, among others. In fact, this structure may incent the advisor to convert more of a family's relationship to an advisory model. There may be a conflict of interest in encouraging a family to sell concentrated positions that are not subject to advisory fees.

ASSET ALLOCATION AND PORTFOLIO CONSTRUCTION CONSIDERATIONS

Once the team has learned all essential information about a family and determined the appropriate set of goals for each account, a team can develop an asset allocation strategy. They may create an overarching strategy and substrategies for each account.

Strategic asset allocation requires a thoughtful analysis of investor and the underlying asset classes. It should be based on an in-depth discussion of an investor's return expectations, risk appetite, time horizon, and cash-flow needs. Strategic asset allocation should establish a long-term (10 to 20 years) view of capital allocation. Plan to revisit this periodically. Unless material changes occur, the allocation should serve as a long-term road map.

Asset allocation and portfolio construction should be carefully coordinated. Too often, I have seen advisors spend a lot of time determining the appropriate asset allocation for a particular client and then assemble a lineup of managers or funds that then implement the strategy in a haphazard fashion. Proper coordination is essential if an overall portfolio is to work as designed. What if managers exhibit style drift or change their approaches over time? Do managers have biases and bets that will alter the allocation? What if market conditions change dramatically?

Asset allocation and portfolio construction considerations are covered throughout this book. This chapter focuses on a few of the key considerations advisors need to account for as part of the overall wealth management process:

- How are you constructing your asset allocation models? By total return or goals-based investing? Strategic asset allocation can be oriented toward generating a total return or designed to meet a specific goal, such as generating income or aligning portfolio and purpose (environmental, social & governance or ESG).

- ○ A total return allocation is designed to optimize the underlying asset classes' returns and risks. Depending on an investor's risk profile and time horizon, different percentages may be allocated to various asset classes. An investor with a healthy risk appetite and a long time horizon may have a higher allocation to equities. Someone closer to retirement and more risk averse may have a higher allocation to fixed income.

- ○ A goals-based investing approach is designed to align with a specific goal, such as accumulating wealth, generating income, or minimizing downside risk. To use this approach, an advisor needs to consistently reinforce and measure progress toward the goals. Don't compare results to the S&P 500 when the portfolio has outperformed and revert to goals-based investing when it lags.

- How do you determine appropriate capital market assumptions? Strategic asset allocation models use return, risk, and correlation data to determine optimal allocations across a range of asset classes. But what if the future is different from the past? What if equity returns and bond yields are lower in the future? What if correlations are higher?

- Do you use some form of tactical allocation? How will you implement it if you do? The markets today are dynamic, and advisors may want to employ some form of tactical overlay to their long-term strategic allocations. This is not an attempt to time the market, but rather to make subtle shifts to better position the portfolio, given the prevailing market environment. Tactics could involve overweighting asset classes that appear undervalued or underweighting asset classes that have run too far, too fast. You could attempt to reduce overall portfolio risk or increase its allocation to an asset class that may benefit from a market change. I would never suggest trying to time the market, but these subtle shifts can add considerable value, especially during volatile times.

- How do you determine asset location across taxable and tax-exempt account types? Allocation across accounts is an important consideration. Many HNW investors may have multiple accounts: an investment account, an individual retirement account (IRA), a 401(k) plan, multiple trusts for the kids, and a private foundation. Each account should have its own asset allocation, and it would be prudent to think about which investments belong in which accounts. Poor asset location decisions could erode the value of a sound strategy by triggering unnecessary tax consequences. The investment account may orient to the long term, to minimize tax consequences. The IRA may hold higher turnover strategies, due to its tax-advantaged status, and the trusts may be geared toward maximizing long-term returns.

- How do you employ active and passive investing? With the prolific growth of ETFs, investors can now efficiently access virtually every market segment in a cost-effective, tax-efficient fashion. However, most traditional ETFs are rules-based, meaning they cannot deviate from their stated screening and weighting methodologies. I believe that there is a role for both active and passive strategies in building portfolios.

- What is the role of alternative investments? Alternative investments represent a broad grouping of underlying strategies, such as hedge funds and private markets. Some are sources of incremental return. Others are alternative income sources, and still others can dampen portfolio volatility.

- Do private markets (e.g., private equity, private credit, and real assets) make sense in today's market environment? Private markets have long been the exclusive domain of family offices, UHNW families, and large institutions.

These strategies are now becoming more accessible for HNW investors at lower minimums and greater liquidity.

CASE STUDY: A CLIENT'S PERSPECTIVE ON SELECTING AND ENGAGING ADVISORS

I often receive questions from advisors regarding dealing with UHNW families. How are they different from HNW families? What unique issues do they face? How do they select and engage their advisors? The following case study addresses these issues.

David Manning (not his real name) and his brother sold their consumer goods business to a large conglomerate for $2 billion. Several advisors at large Wall Street firms, national bank and trust companies, and independent RIAs courted David aggressively. David decided to maintain relationships with Morgan Stanley, Goldman Sachs, and JP Morgan. He wanted access to the best ideas, and he recognized that establishing relationships with these firms meant he would receive preferential access to private equity, private real estate, and other opportunities.

David had built a successful business and now had more money than he could spend. He was in no rush to invest. David had done some estate planning before the sale, but he wanted guidance about setting up a charitable foundation. He needed to set money aside for taxes, and he put the bulk of his money in municipal bonds while he contemplated investment options.

David wanted to understand each firm's strategies and recommended investments, and he chose to hold off on allocating capital until he understood everything. This began a yearlong process with David: reviewing his goals for his various entities, explaining investment theory, reviewing underlying traditional and alternative investments, analyzing historical results, and establishing a way to measure success.

As David became more comfortable, he asked me to review the Goldman Sachs and JP Morgan investments. He was not looking to replace them; instead, he wanted to make sure that the firms were not working at cross-purposes. David wanted an overarching strategy, and he wanted to leverage the best investment options from three of the preeminent firms in private wealth management.

After nearly a year, David began to allocate money across the three firms in a measured fashion. He wanted a team of specialists working hard to earn his trust and his business. In some respects, David was testing us: Were we willing to commit the time and energy to develop a relationship? Or were we motivated by making money? I suspect that many firms would have pushed David to allocate more rapidly, to generate revenues.

David was very bright and asked a lot of good questions about investing, how firms conduct due diligence, potential conflicts of interest, and how advisors were compensated. David asked these questions directly, but I think most wealthy families have similar concerns and try to figure things out on their own. I encourage advisors to proactively address these issues with families. If your goal is to become a trusted advisor, you must be transparent with your clients.

David later asked me to go through a similar educational process with his sister, because I had earned his respect and trust. David eventually set up a family office and asked that I work with his CIO to explain the approach we had developed. Periodically he asked for my opinion on investments, specific funds, and managers. Though David built his family office to focus specifically on the family's needs, he continued to engage a network of trusted advisors in an unbundled fashion, fulfilling specific investment, tax, and philanthropic needs.

I really enjoyed working with David. He was tough and expected a lot of his teams, but he also appreciated the value and expertise we contributed. There are several important lessons from this case study:

- David wanted to develop relationships based on trust and experience.
- David wanted to understand the strategy. He wanted education, not a sales pitch.

- David recognized the value of having advisors compete for his business, getting their best ideas and insights from a broader team.
- David recognized the value of having a team of experts who were willing to work with other trusted advisors.
- David understood that he needed a cohesive strategy that leveraged multiple experts, not multiple competing strategies potentially working at cross-purposes.

HOW DO YOU ADD VALUE?

This chapter describes the evolution from stockbroker to wealth advisor and the ways that advisors engage their clients. Wealth advisors have had to dramatically expand their knowledge of wealth management issues and investment strategies, as well as evolvetheir practices to serve the needs of HNW investors.

Do your clients appreciate your transformation? Can they describe what you do and how you add value?

It might be revealing to sit down with your best clients and ask them to describe your value proposition. How do they describe your capabilities? "Jim helps me pick the best stocks or mutual funds," or "Jim helps me think through my family's goals and objectives. He regularly meets with me and my other trusted advisors to provide comprehensive advice including estate planning, tax management, charitable giving, and investment management."

You have likely spent considerable time defining your value proposition. Do your clients see you the way you want to be seen? Do they think that your value is in outperforming the market? Do you think that is an appropriate way to measure success?

You could frame your value proposition more formally by forming an advisory board comprising a handful of clients. Ask them to help define your value proposition and perhaps even discuss how to grow your practice. Your clients would then be better aligned with your success and would be motivated to help you grow your practice. By forming an advisory board, and inviting some clients to that board, you change the way they think about you and give them a way to advocate on your behalf.

Before launching my new firm, I formed an advisory board composed of like-minded industry leaders. They helped me shape my messaging, my client segmentation strategy, and my reach by providing valuable referrals. Similarly, I try to help my advisory board members by making introductions and sharing my expertise as appropriate. My advisory board encouraged me to write this book.

As an industry, we need to help investors distinguish between the various firms and advisory practices. We need to reshape the way that many investors view financial institutions and recognize the value that a good advisor provides. In his book *Goals-Based Wealth Management*,[4] Jean Brunel suggests that advisors should become interpreters and educators. Brunel recognizes how confusing our industry jargon can be to clients at all wealth levels. He suggests spending the time to educate clients about basic concepts, including modern portfolio theory, the efficient market theory, capital market assumptions, and more. You may even want to suggest a reading list for your clients. More money does not always mean more sophistication. Financial markets are complex, and the media often creates more confusion by overhyping market-moving events.

Another consideration is the role and use of technology: Is it friend or foe? Although technology can provide scale and efficiency, an algorithm lacks empathy and can't read nonverbal cues. HNW families need customized support and services tailored to their needs, not cookie-cutter solutions. You should embrace technology as valuable tools, not as a replacement for your expertise and experience. Help clients by clearly articulating your value proposition.

We all recognize the flaws of chasing performance and allowing investors to define your success or failure relative to some arbitrary benchmark. You might be able to outperform the market, but at what price? Is that what you were trying to accomplish? Clearly, everyone would be better served by moving clients to focus on their progress relative to goals.

A good advisor adds a considerable amount of value beyond performance. A partial list of the services and value that can distinguish one advisor from the next includes:

- **Access to unique investments:** alternative investments, private equity, private credit, and real assets.
- **Experienced team:** familiarity with the complexities facing HNW and UHNW families and the ability to coordinate with other trusted advisors.
- **Access to subject matter experts (SMEs):** in such diverse areas as executive compensation, trust and estate, tax management, charitable giving, and investment management.
- **Educator/teacher:** investors can benefit from your wisdom on a multitude of issues.
- **Coverage model:** a team of experts providing dedicated support and a practice size that allows for proper engagement.
- **Behavioral coach:** helping clients make rational decisions and avoid acting on emotional impulses.

You may need to do a better job articulating how you add value and reinforce that value over time. You need to move the discussion beyond the portfolio to all the services you provide to your clients. You may want to adopt a goals-based approach with HNW investors. Otherwise, you risk being replaced by a robot that is ill-equipped to deal with the complexities of HNW families. A robot cannot see how your client describes the desire to care for his special-needs child or her elderly parent. A robot lacks empathy and emotion, and it cannot pick up on the nonverbal cues that you see instantly.

The industry has evolved a great deal over the past two decades. Many advisors have evolved to become wealth advisors, but some have failed to keep pace with the industry and continue to push products. With increased commoditization and fee compression, you need to be able to articulate and reinforce your value proposition, so you can thrive in the years to come.

CHAPTER 3

Becoming a Behavioral Coach

Our comforting conviction that the world makes sense rests on a secure foundation: our almost unlimited ability to ignore our ignorance.

Daniel Kahneman
Thinking, Fast and Slow

INVESTORS DO NOT ALWAYS ACT RATIONALLY. AFTER ALL, WE ARE only human, and we often respond emotionally to events. Most traditional finance theories assume that people *do* act rationally, considering all available information when they make investment decisions. Behavioral finance challenges that assumption and explores how individuals actually respond to stimuli. It suggests how advisors can help investors make sound decisions.

Harry Markowitz, Bill Sharpe, and Eugene Fama won Nobel Prizes for their work in defining investment theory. Markowitz is generally recognized as the father of modern portfolio theory. Sharpe introduced us to the capital asset pricing model (CAPM), and Fama introduced the efficient market theory. Their research provides the foundation for how we invest today and has spawned numerous other studies and theories. These pioneers in modern finance used historical data to prove their theories. While these theories are highly instructive, they assume that investors make logical and rational choices.

Daniel Kahneman, Richard Thaler, and Meir Statman pointed out the flaws with traditional financial theories, most notably the idea that investors make rational decisions. Kahneman won the Nobel Prize in 2002 for his work identifying a cognitive basis for common human errors that arise from heuristics and biases, and his development of prospect theory, based on loss aversion. Thaler won the Nobel Prize in 2017 for his work researching the interplay of economic and psychology analysis in decision making. Statman's work has focused on investors' cognitive and emotional shortcuts and ways to avoid cognitive and emotional errors.

These behavioral finance pioneers have published extensive research on how investors are wired and why they often make poor decisions. But what can be done about these biases? Can we anticipate these biases and condition investors to do better?

UNDERSTANDING BEHAVIORAL BIASES

The brain is a complex organ that controls all body functions, interprets information from the outside world, and serves as our own supercomputer. Intelligence, creativity, emotion, and memory are a few of the many things the brain governs. The brain receives information through our five senses, often simultaneously. It serves as a supercomputer, assembling and storing messages (Figure 3.1).

The brain also helps us make decisions, often using mental shortcuts, rules of thumb known as *heuristics*. Unfortunately, we all suffer from cognitive biases that cause us to make illogical decisions. Behavioral finance studies the biases and traps that we all fall into when we let our emotions override rational reactions to events. Those traps include:

FIGURE 3.1 **The Original Personal Computer**

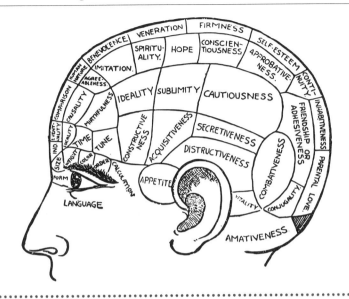

- **Loss aversion.** Investors will go to great lengths to avoid losses. Consequently, they may fall short of their goals by being too conservative.
- **Confirmation bias.** People are often drawn to information or ideas that validate their beliefs and opinions. This bias can hurt investors, who should objectively evaluate a strategy or investment product.
- **Mental accounting.** This occurs when a person views some money sources as different from others—for instance, money you've earned versus money you inherited. Investors may also become emotionally invested in individual stocks or mutual funds.
- **Illusion of control bias.** This occurs when investors believe they can pick individual stocks or managers that will outperform. They believe that because they are in control, the outcome will be better.

- **Recency bias.** Many investors are prone to chasing hot stocks, asset classes, and asset managers. They see strong recent results and extrapolate those results into the future, which rarely works out in the long run.
- **Hindsight bias.** This occurs when investors say (after the fact) that they knew a particular stock or investment would fail. Both investors and advisors tend to overstate their abilities to predict the future, which can lead to excessive risk-taking.
- **Herd mentality.** Although many people pride themselves on thinking independently, humans are social animals and often do what others have done. Investors may chase popular stocks or managers for fear of missing out.

THE IMPACT OF BEHAVIORAL BIASES

Academics have studied behavioral finance and related biases for many years, and wealth advisors have read articles, attended webinars, and heard experts discuss the topic at various industry conferences for decades, but few have effectively incorporated their understanding into their practices. Unfortunately, it is not easy to translate theory into practice, especially when you are dealing with emotional responses. Wealth advisors often exhibit these biases themselves, which may affect the way that clients feel about the markets and their advisors. As shown in Figure 3.2, according to the 2019 BeFi Barometer Survey,[1] advisors identify loss aversion, overconfidence, availability bias, and confirmation bias as their top biases.

These findings are startling and likely shape the way that clients feel about the markets. Based on Kahneman's research, we know that clients exhibit loss aversion as well. Advisors should help them understand that this behavior is irrational and may lead to exiting strategies at precisely the wrong time. However, if an advisor is also concerned about loss aversion, he or she may be more prone to recommend selling positions or becoming more defensive during

FIGURE 3.2 **Advisor's Behavioral Biases**

Advisor Bias	Statements	Agree
Loss aversion	I tend to feel twice as bad about a loss as I feel good about an equivalent gain	82%
Overconfidence	I think my portfolio management skills can help clients outperform the market	65%
Availability bias	I tend to rely on information that is readily available or easily recallable	58%
Confirmation bias	I seek information that confirms my perception or current views	54%
Recency bias	I am influenced by recent news events or experiences when making investment decisions	51%

periods of volatility, when in fact the more prudent approach may be to remain calm and focus on the client's long-term goals and objectives.

Advisors may be overconfident in their portfolio management skills and consequently portray their value proposition as beating the market, something difficult for even the biggest and best managers to do consistently. According to the 2020 SPIVA Scorecard,[2] 67 percent of all mutual funds failed to outperform the broad market over a 1-year period. The longer-term results were more startling, with 71 percent of all funds underperforming over 3 years, 80 percent underperforming over 5 years, and 84 percent underperforming over 10 years. Availability bias and confirmation bias both serve to support the advisor's overconfidence—not a recipe for success.

If we explore applying behavior biases in building portfolios, we should recognize that clients often feel differently about risk in bull and bear markets. During a bull market, clients may say that they are comfortable taking on risk, have a long time horizon, and would be willing to suffer losses in their portfolios.

However, as we experienced during the global pandemic, clients feel very different about risk when volatility emerges. The BeFi Barometer survey asked advisors how they respond to a mismatch in the client's preference and capacity to take on risk. Most advisors (51 percent) create a modified asset allocation strategy based on the client's risk preferences and risk capacity, and only 27 percent adjust their allocation based on behavioral biases. What if clients overstate their willingness to take on risk? What if their time horizons are much shorter than originally stated? See Figure 3.3.

FIGURE 3.3 **Addressing Client's Behavioral Gap When Constructing Portfolios**

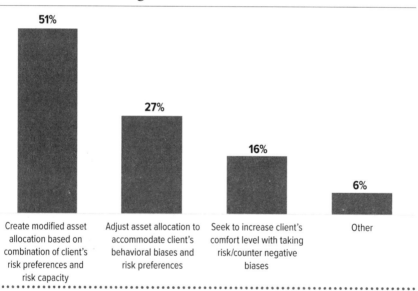

Advisors need to remind clients of their stated goals and objectives, and gauge their feelings about the markets, especially with elevated volatility and uncertainty. Advisors need to protect clients from acting on irrational impulses and ground them in a sound, disciplined process. Sometimes doing the right thing feels uncomfortable, so advisors should prepare clients in advance to avoid emotional responses. An investment policy statement can memorialize this discipline by describing when and how allocations will be rebalanced.

After such a strong bull market (2009–2019), many portfolios likely took on more risk due to market appreciation, and clients may have wanted to let their winners ride. However, advisors who established a disciplined approach to rebalance portfolios when they exceed certain thresholds would have told their clients to trim their equity exposure to align with their stated goals. The investment policy statement can establish the process and avoid the problem of having to convince the client to do the right thing. The rise of discretionary models helps keep clients on the right track, because the advisor does not need permission to do what is appropriate.

Wealth advisors must be sensitive to their own biases, which may shape the way clients view the markets and the advisor value proposition. Advisors should be careful to avoid imposing their biases on clients and focus on adhering to a sound process.

REACTION TO MARKET TURMOIL

We all understand that investors and advisors respond differently to negative shocks than to rising markets. When markets are rising, as they did during the bull market of 2009–2019, investors feel confident and are often willing to take on more risk. Because their portfolios are growing, they may be prone to chasing returns, believing that they can beat the market and confusing skill and momentum. Conversely, during market shocks, as we experienced in February–March 2020, investors are more focused on loss aversion, fearing they may lose their wealth. They are often tempted to sit on the sidelines until the markets stabilize. Of course, both reactions are emotional and introduce different types of risks.

Julie Littlechild, CEO of Absolute Engagement, studied investor behavior between March 10 and March 24, 2020, in the middle of the global pandemic. Based on the timing of this research,[3] the study indicates that larger numbers of clients questioned whether their advisors were providing the guidance they needed. Littlechild's research showed an 11 percent decrease in the number of clients who said they would "definitely" continue to work with their advisors than in the prior year. The change in client loyalty stemmed from gaps in investment performance and risk, overall trust, trust that advisors were putting clients' needs first, and confidence. Clients did not:

- Feel financially secure
- Feel in control of reaching their financial goals
- Feel confident in their ability to reach their financial goals
- Have a clear plan in place to reach their financial goals

Perhaps market turmoil affected the findings. Even so, the results identify areas that advisors should proactively address with clients. Rather than focusing solely on investment results, advisors should reinforce progress relative to a client's stated goals and periodically revisit each client's financial plan to make sure that it reflects the client's current financial circumstances. Advisors should not wait for market-moving events to have these discussions with clients.

Littlechild's research points to the need for better education around the markets as well as issues that aren't market related, including maintaining sufficient assets to meet lifetime income needs (39 percent), coping with a significant market downturn (37 percent), understanding investments or the markets (32 percent), dealing with the rising costs of healthcare and long-term care (29 percent), and ensuring a partner or spouse's financial security if that person is widowed (28 percent). She also noted the need for more relevant engagement with clients—beyond reviewing portfolio returns to engaging clients regarding their needs and desires.

Framing the Discussion

The framing effect describes how we respond to information presentation. We feel positive when we hear, "This new vaccine is 95 percent effective," but feel concerned if we hear, "This vaccine does not provide any benefits 5 percent of the time." The information is the same but our responses are different, and the framing may change our willingness to take the vaccine. Framing can influence investor decision making as well.

The foundational work of psychologists Daniel Kahneman and Amos Tversky explains framing using what they called *prospect theory*. According to this theory, people see a loss as more significant than a gain, and investors will go to great lengths to avoid losses. Kahneman and Tversky's research showed that people will put twice the effort into avoiding loss than they will spend on seeking gain. Because we want to avoid sure losses, we look for options that offer certain gain and avoid options that risk losses.

Framing can influence us to see an opportunity as primarily about gains or mostly about losses. Don't trick an investor, but be cognizant of how clients may respond to framing. Condition investors for the inevitable downturn, rather than focusing only on positive returns and leaving investors unprepared for pullbacks. Discuss both the risks and rewards of investing. I like to tell investors that we are in the risk management business, not the risk avoidance business. There will be market shocks. Our job is to build a portfolio that buffers the impact of these inevitable shocks, while still providing the highest likelihood of achieving the client's goals.

Wealth advisors should be consistent and confident in describing the historical returns and risks of investing, espousing the merits of diversification to help buffer portfolio volatility and providing access to other market segments. Be balanced in discussing the risk-return trade-offs, even though it would be easier to just focus on the positive periods. Investors will appreciate the honesty and will be better prepared for future market shocks.

Use sensitivity in choosing framing options, as well as in visual framing: the way that we present data.

In Figure 3.4, all three lines are the same length, but the arrows create an optical illusion that the middle line is longer. When we present financial data, take visual framing into consideration and recognize that investors may react differently to increasing and

FIGURE 3.4 **Which of the horizontal lines is longest?**

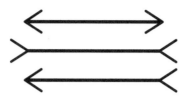

decreasing lines or bar charts. Sometimes it is also effective to high-light focal areas so clients don't gravitate to information that misses the message.

A classic example is a chart showing the growth of $1 million. It shows the growth of indices over an extended time period: the S&P 500, a 60/40 blend, and a global diversified portfolio (Figure 3.5). The investor likely sees a lot of up-and-down periods and big draw-downs during the global financial crisis in 2008. You would like to focus on the advantages of a global diversified portfolio growing over time. How can you better frame the discussion?

Shade the drawdowns and point out the difference between the S&P 500 (down 51 percent) and the 60/40 portfolio (31 percent), and the fact that it takes a 100 percent gain to offset a 50 per-cent decline. Put the cumulative returns of all three lines in dollar amounts. Studies have shown that investors do not relate well to percentage movements, but respond better to dollar results. Walk the investor through the chart, highlighting the value of diversifi-cation in growing the portfolio over time. Point out the cumulative returns, where a $1 million investment in the 60/40 portfolio grew to $2.6 million with a much smoother ride than that offered by only the S&P 500, and a global diversified portfolio grew to $3.1 million due to broader diversification. Proactively address the fact that mar-kets are prone to corrections, by recognizing the drawdown during the global financial crisis and showing how the 60/40 and global diversified portfolios protected investors from big losses during the correction. If you use a handout or a pitchbook, scribble notes highlighting the pertinent information and then leave the material with the investor. Clients remember conversations better if you leave them the marked-up charts.

FIGURE 3.5 **Historical Results of a Diversified Portfolio**

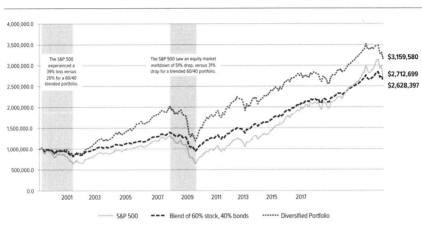

Source: Morningstar Direct. This chart represents a hypothetical investment and is for illustrative purposes only. Data is from January 1, 2001–December 31, 2018. The 60/40 portfolio consists of 60 percent S&P 500, and 40 percent Bloomberg Barclays US Aggregate. Including fees and expenses in the Diversified portfolio would lower returns. The portfolio is rebalanced annually. The global diversified portfolio includes domestic, international, and commodity indexes. Returns include reinvestment of dividends, interest, and capital gains. Indexes are unmanaged, do not incur fees or expenses, and cannot be invested in directly. Past performance is no guarantee of future results.

Another popular chart is the quilt chart, which shows the natural, year-over-year rotation of asset classes, often including a diversified portfolio (Figure 3.6). We refer to it as a quilt chart because of the irregular color patterns showing the best-to-worst-performing asset classes over time. We like this chart because it shows the challenge of trying to select the winners from one time period to the next, and the value of diversification in smoothing the ride. However, investors often see a lot of confusing colors and data. How do you better frame this information?

I like to highlight an asset class such as emerging markets to show the pattern of returns over a given time period. Emerging

FIGURE 3.6 Historical Asset Class Returns (Quilt Chart)

2010	2011	2012	2013	2014	2015	2016	2017	2018	2019
Small Cap Equity 26.85%	US Fixed Income 7.84%	Real Estate 27.73%	Small Cap Equity 38.82%	Real Estate 15.02%	Large Cap Equity 1.38%	Small Cap Equity 21.31%	Emerging Market Equity 37.28%	Cash Equivalent 1.87%	Large Cap Equity 31.49%
Real Estate 19.63%	High-Yield 4.98%	Emerging Market Equity 18.23%	Large Cap Equity 32.39	Large Cap Equity 13.69%	US Fixed Income 0.55%	High-Yield 17.13%	Dev ex-US Equity 24.21%	US Fixed Income 0.01%	Small Cap Equity 25.52%
Emerging Market Equity 18.88%	Gbl ex-US Fixed 4.36%	Dev ex-US Equity 16.41%	Dev ex-US Equity 21.02%	US Fixed. Income 5.97%	Cash Equivalent 0.05%	Large Cap Equity 11.96%	Large Cap Equity 21.83%	High-Yield –2.08%	Dev ex-US Equity 22.49
High-Yield 15.12%	Large Cap Equity 2.11%	Small Cap Equity 16.35%	High-Yield 7.44%	Small Cap Equity 4.89%	Real Estate –0.79%	Emerging Market Equity 11.19%	Small Cap Equity 14.65%	Gbl ex-US Fixed –2.15%	Real Estate 21.91%
Large Cap Equity 15.06%	Cash Equivalent 0.10%	Large Cap Equity 16.00%	Real Estate 3.67%	High-Yield 2.45%	Dev ex-US Equity –3.04%	Real Estate 4.06%	Gbl ex-US Fixed 10.51%	Large Cap Equity –4.38%	Emerging Market Equity 18.44%
Dev ex-US Equity 8.95%	Small Cap Equity –4.18%	High-Yield 15.81%	Cash Equivalent 0.07%	Cash Equivalent 0.03%	Small Cap Equity –4.41%	Dev ex-US Equity 2.75%	Real Estate 10.36%	Real Estate –5.63%	High-Yield 14.32%
US Fixed Income 6.54%	Real Estate –6.46%	US Fixed Income 4.21%	US Fixed Income –2.02%	Emerging Market Equity –2.19%	High-Yield –4.47%	US Fixed Income 2.65%	High-Yield 7.50%	Small Cap Equity –11.01%	US Fixed Income 8.72%
Gbl ex-US Fixed 4.95%	Dev ex-US Equity –12.21	Gbl ex-US Fixed 4.09%	Emerging Market Equity –2.60%	Gbl ex-US Fixed –3.09%	Gbl ex-US Fixed –6.02%	Gbl ex-US Fixed 1.49%	US Fixed Income 3.54%	Dev ex-US Equity –14.09%	Gbl ex-US Fixed 5.09%
Cash Equivalent 0.13%	Emerging Market Equity –18.42%	Cash Equivalent 0.11%	Gbl ex-US Fixed 3.08%	Dev ex-US Equity –4.32%	Emerging Market Equity –14.92%	Cash Equivalent 0.33%	Cash Equivalent 0.86%	Emerging Market Equity –14.57%	Cash Equivalent 2.28%

Source: Callan Associates, 2020

markets is often the best-performing asset class or the worst, and the temptation is to allocate to emerging markets after it has risen dramatically, only to watch it fall precipitously after allocating. I point out that over the long run, emerging markets has been one of the best-performing asset classes, but it provides a bumpy ride. I also point out that the diversified portfolio by definition will never be the top- or bottom-performing asset class. Rather, it holds the various asset classes in optimal weights and serves to reduce the big swings, providing the highest likelihood of achieving the client's goals. Again, I like marking up the chart to draw the investor's attention to the key points.

I often use an analogy to describe asset allocation as getting two things right: selecting the right asset classes and using the optimal combination of asset classes. I have used sports, cooking, and car analogies to bring this concept to life. I find sports analogies helpful, provided the audience understands the sport.

Since my cooking skills are limited, I often use making an omelet to illustrate asset allocation. In making an omelet, it is important to have the right ingredients, in the right proportions. In my omelet, I like eggs, cheese, onions, mushrooms, sausage, and jalapeños. The ingredients are like the asset classes. Not everyone likes jalapeños— like not everyone likes emerging markets, due to the volatility. Therefore, it's important to use the right ingredients in the right proportion. Some investors will exclude asset classes, and weights of each asset class will depend on what they are solving for.

The financial industry is filled with confusing terminology and data. Wealth advisors can help clients navigate the noise and confusion by reframing things in terms that clients understand.

RESPONDING TO BEHAVIORAL BIASES

By better understanding behavioral biases, including their own, wealth advisors may be able to improve client outcomes. Advisors must identify these behavioral biases in advance and may need to reframe the way they present information to their clients. As previously discussed, advisors should resist imposing their biases, instead focusing on developing a sound investment plan. Once you've identified a behavioral bias, it may be possible to either moderate or adapt to it so that the resulting financial decisions more closely match the rational financial decisions traditional finance assumes.

Advisors earn their stripes during challenging times. Investors often exhibit the highest level of overconfidence at market peaks and the greatest level of despair at the bottom. The temptation is to take on more risk when you should be reducing it and to head for the exits when you should be seeking opportunities. Advisors can protect their clients from making the wrong decisions at the wrong times for the wrong reasons. Advisors should build portfolios designed to weather volatility and periodically take their clients' pulses by developing a volatility checklist that addresses their clients' risk tolerance, asset allocation, underlying investments, and tax-management strategies. Consider this market volatility checklist:

- **Review investors' risk tolerance.** If investors are fretting about the market environment, they may be exposed to too much risk. Consider de-risking the portfolio.
- **Review asset allocation.** During times of strong equity returns, allocations may be misaligned with investors' long-term allocation targets. Rebalancing may be appropriate.
- **Review underlying investments.** Make sure that each investment is fulfilling its purpose in the portfolio and that collectively the risk profile is appropriate to the client's goals.
- **Consider tax-management strategies.** You do not need to wait until year-end to consider tax implications.
- **Consider tactical shifts.** To better weather a storm, consider increasing allocations to defensive assets such as cash or gold, or introduce new strategies to buffer volatility.

BECOMING A BEHAVIORAL COACH

Wealth advisors provide valuable advice regarding a myriad of issues facing HNW investors. One of the most valuable roles they play is serving as a behavioral coach, helping investors deal with their irrational impulses to changing market conditions. A behavioral coach is both a psychologist and teacher, diagnosing each client's behavioral biases and educating them to avoid the emotional responses.

Advisors need to see how each client responds to market movements. How do they respond to elevated volatility? Some clients become apprehensive at the first sign of market volatility and need constant reassurances that their portfolio is built to weather the shock. Others are more comfortable with elevated risk and can ride out volatility with little or no intervention. Advisors need to tailor the type, tone, and frequency of communication for each type of client. For the jittery client, frequent communication designed to calm emotional impulses may be appropriate. For the confident client, frequent communicate may signal that they should be more concerned about the markets.

Becoming a behavioral coach needs to start well before a market shock. An advisor needs to establish credibility and gain the client's respect beforehand by explaining how the markets work by balancing return and risk. Earning the client's trust begins with the discovery process, by explaining why you are asking the questions and how you use their answers to build the appropriate portfolio for them. You are trying to ascertain the client's ability to take risk (mathematically) and their willingness to take on risk (emotionally). These will not always match. An HNW investor may have significant wealth, a long-term horizon, and relatively low cash-flow needs, suggesting that the investor can assume a high level of risk. However, in probing deeper, you learn that the investor's father lost his life savings by investing in limited partnerships in the early 1980s and the investor is leery of making the same mistake.

Vanguard has attempted to quantify an advisor's alpha,[4] breaking out such value-added elements as asset allocation, cost-effective implementation, rebalancing, asset location, and behavioral coaching. Their research estimates that in aggregate, an advisor can add roughly 300 basis points, with effective behavioral coaching adding 150 of those basis points. In other words, coaching is the biggest single source of value in an advisor relationship, representing about one-half of all of the value added. Intuitively, this makes sense, because we understand the cost of making irrational decisions and the value of keeping clients engaged when things feel the most uncomfortable.

Asking the Right Questions

To better understand how an investor really feels about the markets and the related risks, it is important to ask the right questions. Ask these questions during the initial discovery process. Revisit the conversation periodically, especially during periods of high volatility.

- How did you feel during the March 2020 market volatility? Did you consider changes in your portfolio?
- How do you feel about your current asset allocation? Do you feel comfortable that you will achieve your long-term goals?
- What is more important to you: outperforming the market in rising markets or retaining your wealth in falling markets?
- What would you do if your portfolio rose 10 percent (increase equity allocation, decrease equity allocation, or keep the same allocation)?
- What would you do if your portfolio fell 10 percent (increase equity allocation, decrease equity allocation, or keep the same allocation)?
- How do you define risk (in traditional financial measures or personal terms)?
- Which would you prefer: a portfolio with lower risk and lower return, or one with higher risk and higher return?

Wealth advisors should educate their clients about the financial markets, asset allocation, and behavioral finance. They should comfort clients by assuring them that they are not alone—everyone is prone to responding to emotional stimuli—and should not shy away from recognizing the challenges in overcoming irrational impulses.

BEHAVIORAL PORTFOLIO THEORY

Building on modern portfolio theory (MPT), Hersh Shefrin and Meir Statman developed an approach that incorporated aspects of MPT and behavioral finance. Behavioral portfolio theory[5] (BPT) moves beyond mean-variance optimization (MVO) and recognizes that investors are not always motivated by maximizing returns. BPT acknowledges that investors are often solving for multiple goals simultaneously. BPT shows investors solving for their needs as a pyramid of mental accounts. Similar to Maslow's hierarchy of needs, BPT's base involves meeting the most basic needs: safety and security. The pyramid's top involves meeting aspirational goals, such as charitable giving. See Figure 3.7.

There are a number of stark differences between MPT and BPT. MPT relies upon MVO to find combinations of portfolios that maximize returns for a unit of risk or minimize risk for a given unit of return. BPT solves for specific needs in a layered approach. MPT views a family as a single portfolio, and BPT recognizes that families are often solving for multiple goals.

Statman suggests that investors may have a behavioral wants frontier[6] that focuses on socially responsible investing, patriotism, pride, and avoiding regret. A portfolio may be less efficient than MVO, but satisfies an investor's wants and aligns with their values. We will cover environmental, social, and governance investing later in this book.

BPT sets the foundation for goals-based investing. It addresses some of MPT's inherent limitations and moves the discussion to solving for investor objectives, rather than merely maximizing returns.

FIGURE 3.7 **Behavioral Portfolio Hierarchy**

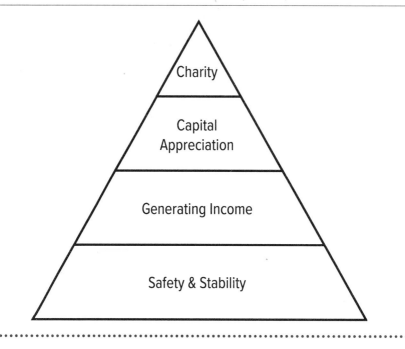

GOALS-BASED INVESTING

Earlier in this chapter, we discussed mental accounting's behavior bias. Investors often view different investments through different lenses, depending on whether an investment sits in the personal, retirement, inheritance, or charity mental buckets. Although mental accounting may have a detrimental effect on decision making, wealth advisors can use goals-based investing to address this bias by dividing a family's goals into targeted buckets.

A family may have multiple short- and long-term goals, including planning for retirement, sending children to college, setting up trusts for children, buying a second home, and establishing a family foundation. Each of these goals has a different time horizon, dollar amount, and capital allocation. See Table 3.1.

TABLE 3.1 **Sample Goals-Based Allocation for an HNW Family**

Goal	Time Horizon	Dollar Amount	Sample Allocation
Retirement	20 years	$5 million	60% equity, 20% fixed income, and 20% alternatives
College (3×)	3–5 years	$2 million	40% equity, 60% fixed income
Trusts (3×)	10 years	$3 million	70% equity, 10% fixed income, and 20% alternatives
Home	1 year	$1.5 million	80% fixed income and 20% cash
Foundation	12 years	$1 million	75% equity, 20% alternatives, and 5% cash

By placing these goals into discrete buckets, we keep the investor focused on what each pool of money is designed to do, then track progress relative to each goal. The strategy plays into the way that investors compartmentalize their investments and provides a higher likelihood of achieving goals, if wealth advisors can adjust and manage toward meeting those goals. Allocations may change as you get closer to reaching the goals, and wealth advisors may need to change the underlying investments to stay on target.

CONCLUSION

Managing client emotions can be as challenging as managing a portfolio and is important work that advisors should be doing with each of their clients. It must begin with the discovery process, as the advisor establishes trust and credibility, and continue as the relationship grows over time. Prepare clients for the inevitable by discussing the market's risks and long-term historical returns. Be mindful of your own behavioral biases and the effect these have on clients.

Carefully consider the words and data you choose to illustrate results. Consider ways to frame the discussion more effectively. Avoid jargon and confusing terminology, and use simple language whenever possible. Use analogies and storytelling to explain complex concepts.

Wealth advisors should embrace their role as behavioral coaches, psychologists, and teachers, preparing clients for market shocks and keeping them engaged when things feel the most uncomfortable. Advisors must protect clients from acting on their emotions and making the wrong decisions at the wrong time for the wrong reasons.

CHAPTER 4

Challenging Modern Portfolio Theory

A good portfolio is more than a long list of good stocks and bonds. It is a balanced whole, providing the investor with protections and opportunities with respect to a wide range of contingencies.

Harry Markowitz

HARRY MARKOWITZ'S DISSERTATION ON PORTFOLIO SELECTION focused on the value of combining two risky investments that do not move in lockstep with one another. Markowitz's cutting-edge research focused on the combination of these investments and concluded that the right combination could in fact produce higher returns at lower risk. He famously stated that "diversification is the only free lunch in investing." We serve the free lunch by properly diversifying investments that show low correlation to one another.

This is the basis of modern portfolio theory (MPT). Markowitz is typically referred to as the father of modern portfolio theory, but other pioneers built on his original work, including Bill Sharpe and Eugene Fama. Sharpe developed the capital asset pricing model

(CAPM) and the Sharpe ratio, which measures risk-adjusted results. Fama is often referred to as the father of the efficient market hypothesis (EMH). Markowitz and Sharpe won Nobel Prizes in economics in 1990; Fama won in 2013.

For the past 30 years or so, advisors have incorporated Markowitz's work into mean-variance optimization (MVO) models, which help advisors build diversified portfolios. Markowitz's work helped transform the way advisors engage their clients, focusing their attention on portfolio outcomes rather than picking individual stocks. In 1952, Markowitz did not have access to the powerful computers that advisors now have at their fingertips. Now wealth advisors can optimize a myriad of asset classes, considering their respective return, risk, and correlation statistics in a matter of seconds.

I have had the opportunity to spend time with Harry Markowitz multiple times over the years and asked him about his groundbreaking research. He was always humble about his work and recognized there was a need for further refinement. I recall a Frontier Analytics Advisory Group meeting with Harry, where I posed a question to him about how to model a large, concentrated position; at the time, I was working with many UHNW families who sold their companies. Many of those families had significant wealth tied up in a single position. Without hesitation, Harry slowly rose from his seat and approached an easel conveniently set up in the boardroom. He proceeded to scribble a mathematical formula to model concentration positions and the efficient disposition of the stock, and then conceded that the modeling had certain limitations, including costs, taxes, and restrictions in selling securities. It was a marvel to see Harry's genius at work—I still have his scribbled notes in my office (a treasure).

Outside large institutions, asset allocation and MPT received little attention until 1986, when Gary P. Brinson, L. Randolph Hood, and Gilbert L. Beebower released their seminal paper, "Determinants of Portfolio Performance." This study examined 91 large US pension funds from 1974 to 1983, comparing their quarterly returns to those of a hypothetical fund holding the same average asset allocation in indexed investments. The study concluded that asset allocation explained 93.6 percent of the variation in a portfolio's quarterly returns.

This study emphasized making sound asset allocation decisions, rather than focusing on security selection or market timing. Academics and practioners have quibbled with the study's robustness and how the results have been marketed, but there is little disagreement that asset allocation is a critical component in achieving long-term goals. Asset allocation has become a cornerstone of an advisor's value proposition, regardless of the methodology used to come up with the optimal combination of asset classes.

CHALLENGING MODERN PORTFOLIO THEORY

MPT assumes that investors are risk averse, and that a rational investor will not invest in a portfolio if a second portfolio offers less risk and the same or better return.

MPT has inherent limitations: investors are not always rational, and they do not always select the less-risky portfolio. Investors often chase returns, gravitating to a hot manager or asset class, especially during bull markets. Markets are not always efficient, and they are prone to boom-and-bust periods, where emotions shift from euphoria to fear. MVO models use long-term capital market assumptions, but returns, risks, and correlations are not stable over the long run.

This chapter addresses some limitations of MPT and evaluates alternative techniques for allocating capital. It delves into the following issues:

- What asset allocation approaches can wealth advisors use?
- What limitations does each approach have?
- How should wealth advisors evolve their approach?
- What is the appeal of a goals-based approach?

ALTERNATIVES TO MODERN PORTFOLIO THEORY

Post-MPT theory came along in 1991, in response to some of the limitations with MPT. This portfolio optimization methodology uses the downside risk of returns instead of the mean variance of investment returns that MPT uses. Both theories describe how to value risky assets and how rational investors should use diversification to achieve portfolio optimization. The difference lies in each theory's definition of risk and how that risk influences expected returns.

Black-Litterman came on the scene in 1992, when Fisher Black and Robert Litterman tried to address some of MPT's limitations, most notably that future returns may be different from historical results. The Black-Litterman model starts with an asset allocation that is based on the equilibrium assumption (assets will perform in the future as they have in the past), and then modifies that allocation by considering projections of future asset class performance.

Liability-driven investing is a common approach to dealing with defined-benefit pension plans, because the liabilities are defined and predictable. It is designed to match a plan's income needs with the appropriate asset allocation. Alternatively, it can work to match HNW investors' yearly cash-flow needs.

Risk parity is a portfolio allocation strategy that uses risk to determine allocations across various components of an investment portfolio. Risk parity builds on MPT, making allocations based on predetermined risk and return targets. Risk parity is used primarily by hedge funds and institutions.

Goals-based investing combines attributes of MPT and behavioral finance by solving for an HNW investor's goals, rather than maximizing returns or minimizing risks. Goals-based investing moves the discussion from beating the market to funding family needs. It focuses on making ongoing progress toward agreed-upon goals.

Critics point to MPT's limitations, but many of the alternative asset allocation methodologies have drawbacks as well. Table 4.1 identifies the limitations of these alternative methodologies. For MPT and post-MPT, the biggest limitation is the robustness and accuracy of the data used to optimize. Using only long-term historical averages of the underlying asset classes may be a flawed approach if future results are dramatically different than the long-term historical data. Black-Litterman seeks to address these limitations by using projections of future results, but what if they are also flawed?

TABLE 4.1 **Asset Allocation Methodologies**

Methodology	Approach	Limitations
Modern Portfolio Theory (MPT)	MPT optimizes a combination of asset classes to maximize the return for a given level of risk or minimize the risk for a given level of return.	Depends on robustness and accuracy of capital market assumptions (return, risk, and correlations). This method assumes that investors select the best long-term portfolios, rather than the highest-returning portfolios now.
Post-MPT	Post-MPT builds on MPT, focusing on optimizing a portfolio's downside risk, rather than the mean variance of returns.	Depends on robustness and accuracy of capital market assumptions (return, risk, and correlations). Post-MPT reduces overall portfolio risk, but may lag in rising markets.
Black-Litterman	Black-Litterman builds on MPT, focusing on the equilibrium assumption and incorporating projections of future results.	Model portfolios may be subject to estimation errors, which may lead to dramatically different results over time.
Liability-Driven Investing	Liability-driven investing is designed to match future flows to future liabilities by size and duration.	This is typically an institutional approach used for defined benefit plans with predictable cash-flow needs.
Risk Parity (Risk Premia Parity)	Risk parity focuses on allocating equally to risk (as defined by standard deviation) across asset classes.	Risk parity helps limit risk, but this approach will likely lag in rising markets, where investors are rewarded for taking on risk.
Goals-Based Investing	Goals-based investing solves for individual investors' goals, such as accumulating wealth, saving for a home, sending a child to college, or generating retirement income.	Investors are prone to chasing returns, and it can be challenging to keep them focused on their goals. Revisit goals periodically, as they may change over time.

Flawed capital market assumptions hurt all the approaches in Table 4.1, as well as the results they produce. Merely using long-term historical averages may lead to higher expectations for returns and income than may be achievable today. Plus, with elevated correlations, investors may not achieve the desired diversification benefits.

Although MPT, post-MPT, and Black-Litterman are somewhat similar in approach, the nuances of each lead to different portfolios. Liability-driven investing and risk parity are more institutional approaches and may not be the best approach for HNW families. Goals-based investing has become increasingly popular because it aligns with investors' goals and objectives, although consistently reinforcing progress relative to these goals can be challenging, given investors' fixation on short-term results.

As we will cover shortly, correlations across asset classes have been rising over the last decade, due in part to increased connectivity between markets. Global synchronized central bank intervention has created a flood of liquidity. Markets react very differently to normal and turbulent periods. Correlations are much more stable over longer market cycles. However, during market shocks, such as those in the second half of 2008, the fourth quarter of 2018, or during the global pandemic, correlations rise significantly. It may be prudent to employ some form of tactical approach during turbulent times, when markets do not act rationally.

The S&P 500's historical annual return has been 10.2 percent from 1956 to 2020. However, according to J.P. Morgan's long-term capital market assumptions, US large-cap equity returns will be 4.1 percent over the next 10 to 15 years, with investment-grade bond returns projected at 2.5 percent and cash at 1.1 percent—all well below the long-term historical average. Table 4.2 shows select long-term capital market assumptions. The lower assumptions are driven largely by the current global economic environment and projections for stunted future global growth.

Capital market assumptions (CMAs) used in models, asset allocation, and financial planning models influence all the approaches listed in Table 4.1. If the difference between the historical averages and

TABLE 4.2 **Select Long-Term Capital Market Assumptions (10–15 years)**

Asset Class	2021 Long-Term Capital Market Assumption	2020 Long-Term Capital Market Assumption
US Small Cap	4.6%	6.5%
US Large Cap	4.1%	5.6%
High-Yield Bonds	4.8%	5.2%
US Treasuries (Intermediate)	1.5%	2.7%
US Investment-Grade Bonds	2.5%	3.4%
Cash	1.1%	1.9%

Source: J.P. Morgan Asset Management Multi-Asset Solutions, 2020, https://am.jpmorgan.com/content/dam/jpm-am-aem/global/en/insights/portfolio-insights/ltcma/ltcma-full-report.pdf

CMAs were small (a few basis points), it would not matter as much as the difference that most firms project today. However, the differences between the long-term averages and the forward-looking projections are quite large. The inputs used in the various models determine the return expectations, income levels, and risk required to achieve client goals over a determined time horizon. Relying on flawed CMAs may lead to overestimating returns, falling short of investor expectations, or being forced to extend time horizons to achieve results.

Wealth advisors need to expand their playbook beyond traditional stock and bond allocations to help clients achieve their long-term goals. Private equity may provide higher returns, private credit provides alternative sources of income, and hedge funds have historically delivered diversification relative to traditional investments. (J.P. Morgan projects a private equity illiquidity premium of 370 basis points.) The merits of alternative investments are covered later in this book.

ASSET ALLOCATION CONSIDERATIONS

The world has changed a great deal since Markowitz's paper was published, both in the number of asset classes and the availability of those asset classes. The additional asset classes serve as valuable diversification tools, because globalization by definition means that markets are more interconnected today. The challenge, of course, is optimizing the number of asset classes in the appropriate weight and using current capital market assumptions to provide realistic expectations around returns and risks.

We often use data such as in Figure 4.1 to illustrate the natural rotation of the best and worst asset classes over time. The purpose of the illustration is not to predict the best asset class, but rather to show the value of spreading risk across multiple asset classes. The best-performing asset class in one time period may become the worst in the next; emerging market was the best-performing asset class in 2017 (up more than 37 percent) and the worst in 2018 (down nearly 15 percent).

Robust, reliable data shows the long-term results of US stocks. However, getting long-term data becomes increasingly more challenging as asset classes with shorter histories are introduced: emerging markets (MSCI 1988), small caps (Russell 2000, 1984), value and growth (Russell 1987), real estate investment trusts (FTSE Nareit 1972), hedge funds (HFRI 1992), and private equity (Cambridge 1986). Many newer asset classes have substantially shorter histories. By comparison, S&P 500 data goes back to 1957 and the Dow Jones Industrial Average data goes back to 1885.

To determine the optimal combination of asset classes, many advisors use some form of MVO modeling, where the critical inputs are returns, risk, and correlation of the underlying asset classes. Many models use long-term historical data. But what if future results do not mirror past results? What if returns are lower and risks and correlations are higher? How can investors achieve their long-term goals?

As previously discussed, the current capital market assumptions suggest that it will be much harder to achieve targeted returns and sufficient diversification using only traditional investments. Alternative investments may be valuable tools in addressing the challenges in the current environment. Private equity provides the

FIGURE 4.1 **Select Asset Class Returns (2010–2019)**

Rank	2010	2011	2012	2013	2014	2015	2016	2017	2018	2019
1	Small Cap Equity 26.85%	US Fixed Income 7.84%	Real Estate 27.73%	Small Cap Equity 38.82%	Real Estate 15.02%	Large Cap Equity 1.38%	Small Cap Equity 21.31%	Emerging Market Equity 37.28%	Cash Equivalent 1.87%	Large Cap Equity 31.49%
2	Real Estate 19.63%	High-Yield 4.98%	Emerging Market Equity 18.23%	Large Cap Equity 32.39	Large Cap Equity 13.69%	US Fixed Income 0.55%	High-Yield 17.13%	Dev ex-US Equity 24.21%	US Fixed Income 0.01%	Small Cap Equity 25.52%
3	Emerging Market Equity 18.88%	Glbl ex-US Fixed 4.36%	Dev ex-US Equity 16.41%	Dev ex-US Equity 21.02%	US Fixed Income 5.97%	Cash Equivalent 0.05%	Large Cap Equity 11.96%	Large Cap Equity 21.83%	High-Yield –2.08%	Dev ex-US Equity 22.49
4	High-Yield 15.12%	Large Cap Equity 2.11%	Small Cap Equity 16.35%	High-Yield 7.44%	Small Cap Equity 4.89%	Real Estate –0.79%	Emerging Market Equity 11.19%	Small Cap Equity 14.65%	Glbl ex-US Fixed –2.15%	Real Estate 21.9%
5	Large Cap Equity 15.06%	Cash Equivalent 0.10%	Large Cap Equity 16.00%	Real Estate 3.67%	High-Yield 2.45%	Dev ex-US Equity –3.04%	Real Estate 4.06%	Glbl ex-US Fixed 10.51%	Large Cap Equity –4.38%	Emerging Market Equity 18.44%
6	Dev ex-US Equity 8.95%	Small Cap Equity –4.18%	High-Yield 15.81%	Cash Equivalent 0.07%	Cash Equivalent 0.03%	Small Cap Equity –4.41%	Dev ex-US Equity 2.75%	Real Estate 10.36%	Real Estate –5.63%	High-Yield 14.32%
7	US Fixed Income 6.54%	Real Estate –6.46%	US Fixed Income 4.21%	US Fixed Income –2.02%	Emerging Market Equity –2.19%	High-Yield –4.47%	US Fixed Income 2.65%	High-Yield 7.50%	Small Cap Equity –11.01%	US Fixed Income 8.72%
8	Glbl ex-US Fixed 4.95%	Dev ex-US Equity –12.21	Glbl ex-US Fixed 4.09%	Emerging Market Equity –2.60%	Glbl ex-US Fixed –3.09%	Glbl ex-US Fixed –6.02%	Glbl ex-US Fixed 1.49%	US Fixed Income 3.54%	Dev ex-US Equity –14.09%	Glbl ex-US Fixed 5.09%
9	Cash Equivalent 0.13%	Emerging Market Equity –18.42%	Cash Equivalent 0.11%	Glbl ex-US Fixed 3.08%	Dev ex-US Equity –4.32%	Emerging Market Equity –14.92%	Cash Equivalent 0.33%	Cash Equivalent 0.86%	Emerging Market Equity –14.57%	Cash Equivalent 2.28%

Source: Callan Associates, 2020

opportunity for higher returns, private credit provides an alternative source of income, and certain hedge fund strategies provide diversification relative to traditional investments. We will cover alternative investments in greater detail later in the book.

We divide alternative investments into hedge fund strategies (equity-hedged, event-driven, relative value, macro, and multi-strategy) and private markets (private equity, private credit, and real assets). These versatile strategies can be valuable tools for wealth advisors in building more sophisticated and durable portfolios for HNW investors. In this challenging environment, HNW investors are demanding access to these once-elusive investments.

Hedge funds and private equity exhibit large dispersion of returns from the best- and worst-performing funds, and the relevant benchmarks use universe comparisons of select funds to calculate results, which may suffer from survivorship bias. Hedge fund benchmarks include data only from funds that are still active, and consequentially suffer from survivorship bias. Underperforming funds may close, and their data is removed from the benchmark. Based on this methodology, the benchmarks may overstate returns and understate risks. As we cover later in the book, there is a great deal of dispersion between the best- and worst-performing private equity fund, especially compared to traditional long-only funds.

The correlations among asset classes is the secret sauce of MPT. Unfortunately, correlations are not static, and they have been increasing over the past couple of decades. Figure 4.2 shows that the correlations across asset classes have risen from 2000–2009 to 2010–2020. During the 2000–2009 time period, commodities exhibited a 0.20 correlation to the US equity markets, and global bonds exhibited a 0.14 correlation. These correlations rose to 0.57 and 0.25 respectively just 10 years later. This is due in part to the interconnectivity of the various global markets.

Over the past decade, correlations have increased dramatically across the board. In fact, during periods of shocks such as the second half of 2008, the fourth quarter of 2018, and during the global

FIGURE 4.2 **Select Correlation Data**

Jan. 2000–Dec. 2009					
	US Equity	Global Equity	Global High-Yield	Commodities	Global Bonds
US Equity	1.00				
Global Equity	0.97	1.00			
Global High-Yield	0.66	0.72	1.00		
Commodities	**0.20**	0.29	0.29	1.00	
Global Bonds	**0.14**	0.24	0.34	0.19	1.00

Jan. 2010–Sep. 2020					
	US Equity	Global Equity	Global High-Yield	Commodities	Global Bonds
US Equity	1.00				
Global Equity	0.97	1.00			
Global High-Yield	0.75	0.83	1.00		
Commodities	**0.57**	0.61	0.69	1.00	
Global Bonds	**0.25**	0.34	0.52	0.23	1.00

pandemic, correlations rose among most major asset classes. When we need the benefits of correlations most, they fail to retain their diversification benefits. This supports the argument for spreading the risk to more and different asset classes, including alternative investments.

EVOLVING ASSET ALLOCATION

Harry Markowitz introduced us to the value of diversification in building portfolios, but the world has changed a great deal since Markowitz's seminal work in the 1950s. We need to learn the lessons of history and evolve our approaches to fit the current market environment. We need to expand the number of asset classes to identify opportunities and diversify risk.

As advisors began to educate investors about the benefits of diversification, many adopted the 60/40 allocation as a popular benchmark portfolio, with investors gaining most of their returns from their equity allocations and income primarily from bond allocations. The long-term historical annual average of the S&P 500 is 10.2 percent, and the long-term annual yield on fixed income is roughly 4 percent. The equity allocation provided strong returns, the fixed-income allocation provided income, and together investors achieved some degree of diversification because of their investments' low correlation to one another. The naïve 60/40 portfolio provided attractive returns, income, and diversification, and investors could easily shift their allocations to generate higher returns or to accommodate other needs over time.

But what should advisors do if equity returns and bond yields are lower during the next 10 to 20 years? What if correlations among asset classes remain elevated? How can investors achieve their desired return requirements? Do they need to take on more risk or extend their time horizons?

Advisors should consider broader diversification across their equity and fixed income allocations, including international developed, emerging markets, high-yield bonds, real estate, commodities, and certain types of alternative investments. The broader diversification can help increase return, reducing risk and providing noncorrelating returns. With the strong US equity market returns during the bull run, advisors have been slow to incorporate hedge fund strategies in a meaningful way. Some of this is due to the generally lackluster results of many of these strategies, and some is due to the lack of education and conformity in describing what these strategies are designed to do in a diversified portfolio.

Most hedge fund strategies are not designed to outperform the S&P 500 in a rising market. Strategies such as equity hedge and event-driven hedge their exposure to the market, relative value is a conservative strategy designed to provide steady incremental returns, and macro and multistrategy are defensive strategies that earn their stripes in difficult market conditions. Therefore, benchmarking these strategies relative to the S&P 500 are not meaningful. Private equity, private credit, and real assets are garnering a lot of attention because of their potential return, income, and diversification benefits. These once-elusive asset classes are now available to more investors at lower minimums and with better liquidity.

With traditional returns and income likely well below their historical averages, advisors need to identify alternative sources of returns and income for their clients. They need to evaluate different strategies and structures to meet clients' needs and objectives.

FIGURE 4.3 **Select Asset Class Returns (2000–2020)**

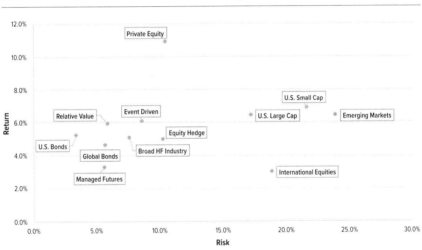

Source: iCapital Network, Hamilton Lane, HFR and Envestnet. Risk and returns data is from January 2000–December 2020.

Private equity historically has delivered strong absolute and relative returns compared to traditional asset classes. Today, there are substantially more private companies than public companies—and many will stay private longer. We cover private equity later in this book.

ASSET ALLOCATION CONSIDERATIONS

There are several asset allocation and portfolio construction considerations in building better portfolios. The following represent a few key issues:

- Strategic versus tactical allocation
- Asset allocation and asset location
- Active versus passive investing
- The role and use of alternatives
- Portfolio construction

Tactical Allocation

Given some of the limitations previously noted, and the dynamic nature of today's market cycles, advisors may want to incorporate a tactical overlay to respond to changing market conditions. I do not recommend making big swings in and out of the market, but rather subtle shifts to better position portfolios, given the prevailing market conditions. I suggest that advisors develop a process to implement and track tactical allocations, including the following:

- How do you make decisions?
- Is there an asset allocation committee?
- What is the rationale for the tactical allocation?
- What would cause you to unwind the tactical allocation?
- What are the offsetting overweight and underweight positions?
- How do you measure success?

Larger firms may have a robust process and a formal governing body (asset allocation council or investment committee). Regardless of firm size, I recommend documenting the process and tracking the results. The frequency and size of the tactical shifts may vary, depending on the prevailing market conditions. For example, after the record bull market run (2009–2019), it may have been prudent to adopt a more defensive posture. This could have been accomplished by reducing exposure to risk assets (domestic and international equity) and increasing exposure to defensive assets (cash, gold, or macro). Tactical allocations could also overweight attractive asset classes (value) and underweight expensive ones (growth).

Asset Location

Advisors often spend a lot of time thinking about client asset allocation strategy, but they spend little time thinking about which investments belong in which type of account (e.g., personal account, retirement account, trust, etc.). Asset location is an important consideration for HNW investors, because the tax consequences of bad decisions may erode any benefit gained from asset allocation.

Consequently, advisors may want to consider ETFs or tax-managed strategies to gain market exposure. ETFs are typically more tax-efficient than most SMAs and mutual funds, and they are typically available at substantially lower costs than either. It may be prudent to hold high turnover strategies in tax-deferred accounts and low turnover strategies in taxable accounts.

Active and Passive

A later chapter covers incorporating active and passive investing, but I will provide a summary here. For ease of understanding, I will refer to ETFs as passive investing, and mutual funds and SMAs as active management, even though there are active ETFs and passive mutual funds. ETFs' appeal is their ability to access virtually any segment of the market in a cost-effective, tax-efficient fashion, with fees approaching zero. ETFs have experienced strong growth at the expense of active managers who failed to outperform their respective benchmarks.

By contrast, active managers claim they can outperform the market by selecting securities. Active managers can also play defense, navigating through challenging market environments, whereas passive strategies can't deviate from their stated disciplines. Active managers may also be the best option in less-efficient asset classes and niche strategies.

Alternative Investments

As discussed here and later, alternative investments are flexible tools in dealing with today's challenging market environment. Hedge fund strategies can be long and short, exploiting market opportunities and deploying capital more efficiently than long-only strategies. Hedge funds can invest in stocks, bonds, commodities, currencies, futures, and options and may use leverage to amplify results. Product innovation has made these strategies more accessible to HNW investors.

Private markets have historically been available only to large institutions and family offices, but with product innovation, regulatory relief, and private equity firms' increased willingness to bring products to HNW investors, these elusive investments are now easier to access than ever. In a lower return environment for most traditional investments, private markets represent attractive opportunities, as private equity has historically achieved a roughly 3 percent illiquidity premium.

Though alternative investments offer attractive returns with potentially lower risks, advisors and investors must carefully consider some of the structural trade-offs. Because these strategies were originally developed for institutions and family offices, they have higher minimums, limited liquidity, and complex fee structures, plus they are generally limited to accredited investors and qualified purchasers.

PORTFOLIO CONSTRUCTION

Asset allocation provides a framework for allocating capital. Portfolio construction is how we put the pieces of the puzzle together. Asset allocation and portfolio construction should be done in conjunction, to ensure that the strategy is properly aligned to meet the stated goals. For example, if your asset allocation calls for a 15 percent allocation to large-cap value, ensure that the mutual fund, SMA, or ETF selected is style pure so you are not taking on unintended bets. The reality is that most mutual funds and SMAs make bets in their attempts to beat the market and may be tempted to buy growth companies when they are in favor or dip down in capitalization to pick up incremental returns.

Though it may seem trivial, style drift changes the portfolio's asset allocation and risk-return profile. In the previous example, if your large-cap value allocation includes large-cap growth and mid-cap stocks to boost returns, you could be introducing considerably more risk to your portfolio and jeopardizing your ability to meet your client's goals. It is not enough to evaluate the returns and risk of a given strategy. Advisors should evaluate the underlying holdings to determine whether the manager is adhering to the stated discipline and spot any style drift. If your asset allocation and portfolio construction do not mesh, there could be considerably more risk than warranted, and you may fall short of meeting your goals.

Factor Investing

Factor investing has become increasingly popular because it lets investors isolate underlying exposures (value, growth, quality, momentum, size, and low volatility) and avoid unintended bets and biases. Institutions have incorporated factor investing for decades, as ample academic research shows the merits and persistence of certain factors. These strategies are now available in ETFs, making it easier for advisors and investors to access and provide an efficient means of building portfolios. Factor investing provides greater precision in aligning asset allocation and portfolio construction. We will cover factor investing in the next chapter.

For managers and strategies that have more freedom in seeking opportunities, dissecting factor exposures may be valuable in understanding the bets and biases. Often managers exhibit multiple factors in their portfolios, sometimes intentional and sometimes a by-product of their discipline. Dissecting individual managers' factors provides a lot of valuable information when evaluating the overall portfolio. Your value manager may be exposed to value, income, and volatility, and your growth manager may be exposed to momentum, quality, and size factors. In combination, these factors may provide market weight exposures.

Structural Considerations

HNW investors often have healthy exposure to alternative investments (hedge funds and private markets), and advisors need to consider the liquidity embedded in the various structures. The classic hedge fund limited partnership structures often have limitations on the amount and frequency of redemptions, and advisors need to take this into consideration before allocating capital. Advisors may want to consider more liquid structures if HNW investors are unable or unwilling to tie up capital for extended periods.

The classic private equity fund is affected by the J-curve. This describes the way capital is drawn down and deployed over the life cycle of a fund, with negative cash flow during the early stages as opportunities are being sourced. Consequently, investors should view private equity as a long-term investment (7 to 10 years). Although there are newer structures coming to the market promising better liquidity, of course there are structural trade-offs, and there is a reason that private equity funds prefer longer time horizons to source and harvest opportunities.

Advisors should take investors' cash-flow needs, and the liquidity available in the various structures, into consideration before allocating to alternative investments. They should evaluate the structural trade-offs, including minimums, fees, and accreditation standards of classic funds and registered funds. We will cover these issues in greater detail later in this book.

Measuring the Results

Once you have developed an asset allocation strategy and assembled the appropriate manager lineup, you need to determine how you will measure the results. I have heard advisors and investors complain about benchmarking for years. Should you use a blended benchmark? Broad market indexes? Should you measure progress relative to the client's goal?

When evaluating results, there are two primary things we measure: Is the overall portfolio meeting our expectations? Are each of the managers and funds fulfilling our expectations? Evaluate managers versus their appropriate benchmarks (S&P 500, Russell 2000, MSCI EAFE, Barclays Aggregate Bond, HFRI, Cambridge Private Equity, etc.). Benchmarks should measure returns and risks. I understand that some firms do not subscribe to the index data and may have to use broad-based benchmarks instead. Advisors may also want to conduct peer group comparisons, evaluating risk and return versus a universe of similar managers or funds.

Wealth advisors also want to evaluate the results of the overall portfolio: Is the asset allocation functioning as designed? Are the pieces of the puzzle assembled appropriately? Is the family getting closer to their goals? Establish review frequency and the appropriate benchmarks to measure the results. Advisors may want to point out benchmark limitations in advance, but must stick with their benchmarks in good periods and bad. Changing benchmarks only erodes the client's trust.

GOALS-BASED INVESTING

I began this chapter by challenging some of the limitations of MPT: the assumption that investors are rational and will select the optimal portfolio, and that they always seek to maximize returns. Goals-based investing has become a mainstream response to the limitations of MPT, incorporating aspects of behavioral finance to solve for investor needs. Goals-based investing is intuitive and easy to explain to investors, and it fits neatly within the consulting process, providing the flexibility to solve for multiple goals simultaneously. Goals-based investing moves the discussion with clients from outperforming the market to progress relative to their stated goals, and it reinforces a long-term approach to investing.

Goals-based investing is a natural response to the limitations of MPT. Rather than maximizing returns or minimizing risks, goals-based investing is designed to provide the highest likelihood of achieving a client's goals over time. While it balances returns and risks, the utility function of goals-based investing is to achieve a desired outcome: capital appreciation, wealth preservation, retirement income, saving for a second home, college funding, or charitable donations.

Because HNW families often have multiple goals across multiple accounts, advisors should determine the specific desired outcomes and establish obtainable goals for each account. Advisors must consistently reinforce progress relative to client goals in rising and falling markets, as well as the predetermined time horizon to achieve those goals. Advisors might be tempted to focus on strong performance in good times and revert to the goals when things are tough, losing credibility with clients and making it difficult to keep them focused on their plans.

CHAPTER 5

Incorporating Active and Passive Strategies

A blindfolded monkey throwing darts at a newspaper's financial pages could select a portfolio that would do just as well as one carefully selected by experts.

Burton Malkiel
A Random Walk Down Wall Street

BURTON MALKIEL'S CLASSIC BOOK LAID DOWN THE GAUNTLET that active managers could not consistently outperform the market. He assumed that the market is efficient and that a security's price reflects all available information about it. Published in 1973 and updated multiple times, *A Random Walk Down Wall Street* has fueled the passive investing revolution, with the first index fund launched by Vanguard in 1975 and the first ETF launched by State Street Global Advisors (SSgA) in 1993.

Today, in the United States alone there are over 1,400 ETFs, representing approximately $5 trillion in assets under management. ETFs have helped *democratize* investing by making it easy to access virtually every segment of the market in a cost-effective, tax-efficient manner. They let investors gain exposure to broad market segments, with no minimums, in a single trade. Before ETFs, investors who wanted to own the S&P 500 had to purchase the underlying securities and assemble them in the same weights the index used. This was very expensive and difficult to accomplish, and market appreciation meant an investor's exposure would typically deviate from the index returns over time. But now in a single trade, it is easy to own the underlying basket, at prices at or near zero, without transaction costs and with built-in automatic rebalancing.

FIGURE 5.1 **The Growth of Passive Investing**

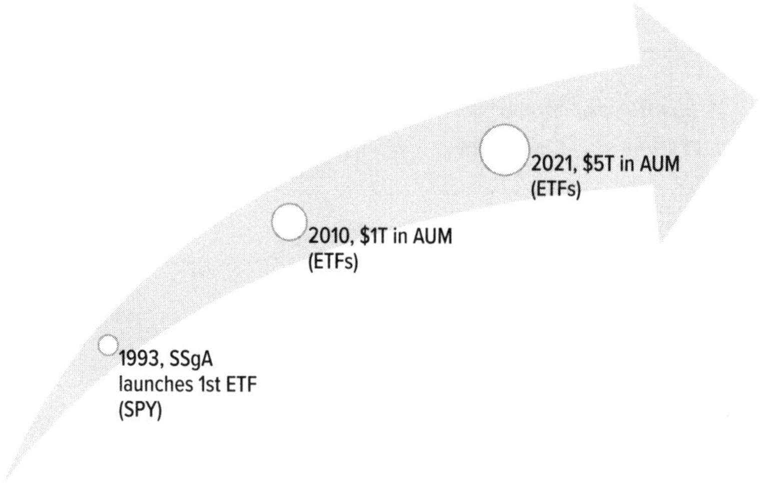

2021, $5T in AUM
(ETFs)

2010, $1T in AUM
(ETFs)

1993, SSgA
launches 1st ETF
(SPY)

For decades investors have debated which is better: active or passive management. Active managers claim to be good at identifying strong and avoiding weak companies. Advocates of passive management point out that active managers don't consistently outperform their benchmarks. In recent years active ETFs and passive mutual funds have blurred the lines between the two camps. There are roles for both active and passive management, which we examine in this chapter.

THE RISE OF PASSIVE

The rise of ETFs accelerated after the 2008 GFC, as many active managers failed to outpace the market and investors revolted against paying high fees for active managers who performed no better than the market. Advisors began to adopt ETFs as building blocks for assembling diversified portfolios, and investors began to dabble in trading ETFs on their own, leading to the rapid growth of ETFs, in both the number of strategies and the assets under management. ETFs have continued to evolve and are now available in various flavors, from "cheap beta" to "smart beta," from strategies designed to mimic a particular index to active ETFs.

Historically, ETF ownership has been fairly evenly split between retail and institutional investors. Hedge funds embraced the ease of owning broad segments of the market, in a tradable structure. They could be long the US markets and short international, or long small-cap stocks and short large-cap stocks, and could easily unwind their trades. Institutional investors use passive strategies in various ways, including expressing tactical views, providing beta exposure, or temporary beta exposure (when seeking a replacement), and overweighting or underweighting factor exposure. Institutions may choose to use ETFs or other index-based strategies to reflect both long- and short-term views of the market. Advisors can use ETFs to reflect their views and biases, by deploying momentum, quality, value-biased, yield-oriented, and low volatility ETFs.

Family offices and UHNW families like the tax efficiency and the flexibility of ETFs. They can easily adjust portfolio exposures and be more nimble in responding to changing market conditions. Retail investors like the ability to efficiently access the markets, and ETFs have quickly become a larger percentage of the daily market volume. Rather than debating the merits of owning Apple, Amazon, or Google, it is now easy to own all three with a simple mouse click.

As the ETF industry has matured, we see several positive developments. The competitive environment has led to a dramatic fee reduction: some ETFs are priced at or near zero. We have seen product innovation, from products designed to mirror the market cheap beta to strategies designed to outperform the market smart beta. To complicate things, there are now active and "nontransparent" ETFs (active strategies that do not provide transparency). ETFs are merely the wrapper that holds the underlying basket of securities.

Some active managers demonstrate skill in selecting securities, but most have a difficult time delivering consistently market-beating results. Annually, S&P produces a scorecard that measures the number of managers that have outperformed the market. The SPIVA Mid-Year 2020 Scorecard[1] showed that an unspectacular 67 percent of active managers failed to outperform the overall market. Growth funds performed well over the one-year period: 74 percent of large-cap growth, 83 percent of mid-cap growth, and 89 percent of small-cap growth funds beat their benchmarks. However, over the long run, 92 percent of large-cap growth, 74 percent of mid-cap growth, and 75 percent of small-cap growth funds underperformed their benchmark over the past 15 years.

This data is significant in that it includes the dramatic downturn caused by the pandemic and the sharp reversal following the injection of fiscal and monetary stimulus. Results for everyone except growth managers were pretty dismal, considering that uncertainty should reward active management. For years, active managers have claimed that they can't outperform in a rising market that's driven by money flowing into passive strategies, but they would outperform when the markets got challenging and they could demonstrate their skill.

ETFs are generally more tax efficient than comparable strategies, because of their cost structure and the unique "creation/redemption" process. The creation/redemption process is the "secret sauce" in providing an ETF's tax efficiency. When investors invest in mutual funds, the manager uses that money to buy securities, paying commissions and incurring spreads that ultimately affect investor returns. When investors withdraw money from the fund, the manager sells securities and may incur tax consequences.

Rather than paying other investors' taxes, as in a mutual fund, an ETF leverages the expertise of authorized participants to create and redeem units. To address increasing demand, an authorized participant creates an underlying basket of stocks, something known as a creation unit, or redeems stocks to facilitate significant outflows. Authorized participants can accomplish this without incurring taxes, because they are creating new units and delivering them to the ETF sponsor.

A quick note on the race to zero: free is not always free. Although a few ETF sponsors now claim to offer free ETFs, a deeper dive can help us understand ETF cost structure and revenue streams. The total cost of ETF ownership includes both explicit and implicit costs. The explicit costs include the operating expense ratio, commissions, trading costs (bid-ask spreads), and discounts and premiums to net asset value (NAV). Implicit costs include tracking error and capital gains. An ETF sponsor may also generate revenue by lending securities.

Killing growth-propelling innovation is a potential unintended consequence of the race to zero. Asset managers are not incented to develop products with little or no revenue. Advisors and investors should demand fair and equitable pricing, but we still pay a price for falling costs and revenues.

The extraordinary growth of ETFs has helped drive mutual fund fees lower over the past several years. This has been a positive development, because their high fees made it challenging for them to consistently outperform the market, like a sprinter who carries extra weight.

THE ROLE OF ACTIVE MANAGERS

Though ETFs have certainly experienced extraordinary growth over the past decade, and some have predicted the demise of active management, mutual funds still represent a primary investment vehicle for investors, with more than 100 million American families and

$21.3 trillion in mutual funds as of year-end 2019.[2] The majority of US mutual fund assets are in equity funds (53 percent), followed by bond funds (22 percent), money market funds (17 percent), and hybrid funds (7 percent). Retail investors hold the majority of assets (89 percent). ETFs have increased their market share, but this is still significantly smaller than that of mutual funds.

In spite of the cited SPIVA data, active managers are better equipped to deal with market uncertainty and can play defense when warranted. Index-based strategies by their very nature must track an underlying index whether the markets are rising or falling. An active manager can adapt to the prevailing market conditions and be more aggressive or defensive, depending on their forward-looking views. Active management also makes sense in less-efficient asset classes (emerging markets), niche strategies (option overlay), alternative investments (hedge funds and private markets), and tax-managed strategies.

Active managers can demonstrate skill in challenging market environments, where there is a bigger difference between winning and losing companies and security selection is at a premium. During the bull market of 2009–2019, momentum stocks dominated the market. Their growth was fueled by money pouring into ETFs, which pushed these stocks even higher. The next 10 years are likely to be different than the previous 10 years, and we may see a market environment that rewards skillful stock pickers. Market cycles tend to ebb and flow, and the next cycle will likely be more discerning in distinguishing between the winners and losers.

Many of the most successful fixed-income ETFs are actively managed, and all fixed-income ETFs have an active element. The fixed-income markets and equity markets are different. If you want to own the S&P 500, you can easily buy an appropriately weighted basket of a finite number of securities. But fixed-income ETFs do not seek to own the same bonds in the same weight as the Barclays US Aggregate Bond Index (the most popular bond index). Rather, they seek to own bonds with similar characteristics to the benchmark (sector, quality, duration, etc.). Many have questioned whether the benchmark is representative and asked why investors would want to replicate the results, leading many investors to favor active investment options.

Many asset managers tout tax management as one the advantages of SMAs versus mutual funds, and ETFs are generally a tax-efficient structure. That said, there are dedicated managers who focus on tax management throughout the year. Tax-managed strategies make a lot of sense for HNW investors. In fact, some of the tax-managed strategies claim to be able to capture after-tax alpha through effective tax-loss harvesting. The focus on managing a portfolio for tax efficiency, and the ability to offset gains and losses, is certainly valuable to HNW and UHNW families. Tax management is of critical importance to wealthy families and should not be taken lightly. Any advisor serving HNW investors should consider some kind of active tax management.

The question is not active versus passive investing, but rather how to use active and passive strategies effectively. The hurdle for active managers is whether they can deliver excess returns after fees and taxes. Skillful managers are available in the marketplace; the challenge, of course, is finding them. Many advisors have decided to devote their time and energy to more value-added endeavors.

If overcoming a higher fee structure is an impediment for active managers, active ETFs are the logical answer. Many large-asset managers have seen significant asset outflows over the past several years. We have seen a number of ETF provider acquisitions thwart the outflows, and several managers have launched their own ETFs. Rather than competing in the race to zero, these newer entrants have gravitated to active, nontransparent, or smart beta ETFs to retain some pricing power.

SMART BETA STRATEGIES

The first generation of index products was designed to mirror an underlying index in a cost-effective wrapper. These products grew in popularity based largely on the ease of accessing various market segments, and active managers' difficulty in consistently outperforming passive benchmarks. As we discussed, ETFs have become a universal tool for advisors, investors, and institutions to build portfolios or access markets. Much of ETFs' growth was at the expense of active managers, as ETFs provided cheap beta exposure.

The first-generation products were primarily market-cap weighted: the largest companies (based on market capitalization) had the largest weight in an underlying index. This is how the most common indexes are constructed (S&P 500, Russell 2000, MSCI EAFE, etc.). The Dow Jones Industrial Average is price weighted: the most expensive company has the largest weight. As ETFs gained popularity, many began to question arbitrarily weighting products in this fashion when a lot of academic research has shown that certain known factors have historically led to outperformance.

Smart beta strategies, also known as strategic beta or alternative beta, have grown in popularity over the past decade or so due to their ability to improve on market results. Many of these strategies have outperformed the market and/or reduced risk relative to the market. Smart beta includes a range of strategies: fundamental, quality, momentum, low volatility, and equal weight to name a few. Many of these strategies deliver excess return by exploiting known factors such as value, size, quality, low volatility, and momentum, while other strategies merely rely on back-tested data that shows strong hypothetical results.

With the proliferation of strategic beta strategies, investment research company Morningstar began tracking the asset flow and number of strategies available to investors, and it introduced a taxonomy to help advisors distinguish between the various types of strategies. As of June 2020, there were 632 exchange-traded products (ETFs and exchange-traded notes), with $869.7 billion in assets under management, representing roughly 20 percent of the $4.38 trillion invested in exchange-traded products.[3] The growth has come primarily from new adopters, many of whom were leaving active management options. Approximately 72 percent of the growth in strategic beta exchange-traded product assets over the past two decades has come from net new inflows, and the remaining 28 percent reflects asset appreciation.

Strategic beta strategies are not homogeneous, with each strategy employing its own screening and weighting methodologies. The difference in approach may lead to dramatic differences in market capitalization, sector bets, value versus growth splits, and risk-return characteristics.[4] Table 5.1 describes a few of the more popular smart beta strategies, their weighting methodologies, and the respective portfolio tilts.

TABLE 5.1 Defining a Few Smart Beta Strategies

Smart Beta Type	Screening and Weighting Methodology	Bias / Tilt
Fundamental	Screens and weights securities based on adjusted sales, cash flow, dividends, and buybacks.	Value-tilting
Quality	Screens and weights securities focusing on companies with strong balance sheets, low debt levels, and strong earnings.	Value/Quality
Momentum	Screens and weights securities based on those companies that have performed well recently (6–12 months).	Growth-oriented
Low Volatility	Screens and weights securities based on those that have historically exhibited low volatility relative to the overall market.	Value-tilt
Equal Weight	All securities are equal weighted initially, with quarterly rebalancing back to equal weight.	Small-/mid-cap bias

Because of the difference in screening and weighting methodologies, these strategies move in and out of favor over time. Momentum is a growth-oriented strategy that performed well from 2015 to 2020, with the dominance of the FAANG stocks (Facebook, Apple, Amazon, Netflix, and Google). Conversely, fundamental is a value-tilting strategy that lagged as value dramatically underperformed growth over the past decade. Advisors and investors should understand the built-in biases before investing in smart beta strategies.

Factor Investing

The industry often uses "strategic beta" and "factor investing" interchangeably, but not all strategic beta strategies are based on factor research. The term *factor* describes characteristics of a group of securities that can explain return and risk. In recent years, a plethora of new strategies has come to market, all claiming to have identified new factors. MSCI has conducted extensive research on factor investing and offered the following perspective:

> While many factors have been shown to have statistical significance in explaining variations in risk and returns, not all these factors offer risk premia relative to CAPM pricing. Risk premia factors are those which represent exposure to systematic sources of risk that have historically earned a long-term premium. We have so far identified six risk premia factors: Value, Low Size, Low Volatility, High Dividend Yield, Quality and Momentum. These factors have been empirically tested in years of academic research and there are solid explanations on why they have historically provided risk premia.

Factor investing dates to the 1960s, following the introduction of the capital asset pricing model (CAPM), which describes the relationship between systematic risk (i.e., volatility) and expected returns. Eugene Fama and Kenneth French built on CAPM, introducing their three-factor model in the 1990s, which added size and value factors to the market risk factors in CAPM. Research on factor investing is extensive, going back decades, and large institutional investors have used factor investing for decades. Today ETFs can capture these factors in rules-based structures, so they are easily accessible now to advisors and investors.

As factor investing has become more widely accepted, we have seen a proliferation of multifactor strategies coming to the marketplace. Multifactor strategies allocate across multiple factors: value, quality, momentum, and low volatility. These strategies can be static (maintaining a target allocation) or dynamic (shifting allocation based on the prevailing market conditions). These strategies appeal to investors by capturing the natural rotation of factors moving in and out of favor. But do they add value above and beyond owning the market? Do they cancel out the benefits of isolating the factor exposures in a portfolio? I believe in the value of factor diversification. Advisors can either do it on their own with the numerous factor ETFs available today or allocate to a multifactor ETF that allocates based on its own methodology.

THE RISE OF THE MODELS

A new type of active management is beginning to gain traction: asset allocation models that use ETFs, mutual funds, and SMAs as building blocks to gain exposure to market segments. Asset managers, wealth advisors, and the home offices of many of the large wealth management firms are developing these models. Because of the abundance of raw materials, both the number and the diversity of models have grown substantially, solving for everything from total return to specific goals.

Although asset allocation model portfolios have been around since the early 1990s, they have evolved a great deal over the past couple of decades, due in large part to ETF diversity. The first generation of models primarily used mutual funds or selected individual securities. ETFs have dramatically expanded the toolbox, making it easy to access markets and alter weighting methodologies to provide different outcomes. Asset allocation models can represent a total portfolio solution or a specialized sleeve.

Asset managers have seized the opportunity to leverage their expertise and capture a significant portion of the overall portfolio allocation. This helps staunch the bleeding of assets from mutual funds and SMAs, as well as fee compression across the industry. Leveraging third-party models can free up advisors to focus on other wealth management issues and deepen their relationship with HNW families, as well as help investors receive dedicated portfolio management and the broader set of wealth management solutions they need.

Models can include mutual funds, ETFs, or individual securities across a broad array of asset classes. Home-office staff have embraced models because they let advisors spend more time on broader wealth management issues and focus on the overall client experience. Wealth advisors like having the ability to serve as the quarterback, determining the client's needs and objectives, and selecting the appropriate model to reach client goals. If the investors goals change or the model falls short of expectations, the advisor can easily replace the model. Table 5.2 outlines the value and limitations of models among the three key stakeholders: asset manager, advisor, and investor.

Similar to the SMA business in the early 1990s, asset allocation model portfolios represent a way to leverage the expertise of third-party asset managers and better align advisors' interests with those of their clients. Models give asset managers a way to capitalize on their expertise and own a larger slice of the pie. They let advisors align their interests with those of their clients and tap into the expertise of world-class asset managers. Investors gain access to a more specialized team of experts.

Many advisors believe that their value proposition is enhanced by creating portfolios. But according to Cerulli Research Reports, just 28 percent of investors believe their advisors have the highest level of investment expertise, and 35 percent prefer a dedicated investment team. Investors' value a team of dedicated professionals, each with their area of expertise: investment management, financial planning, trust and estates, philanthropy. The wealth advisor's value is in assembling the team and accessing these resources as appropriate.

The challenge for many advisors is effectively pivoting, especially if they have positioned their value proposition as building portfolios. For advisors who have moved significant assets to "Rep-as-PM" or "Rep-as-Advisor" programs, this may be a more challenging discussion. It may be more appropriate to position models as a complementary solution, as their value proposition has likely been acting as portfolio manager.

TABLE 5.2 **Value and Limitations of Models**

	Value of Models	Limitations of Models
Asset Manager	Allows asset managers to leverage their expertise and capture a larger slice of the pie. Models also help move the discussion beyond the performance of an individual sleeve, and focus attention on model performance	Models still need to deliver the results: return, income, risk, and desired outcome. Other asset managers and home offices provide a lot of competition.
Advisor	Models let advisors devote more time and energy on other wealth management issues (financial planning, retirement planning, trust and estate, lending, philanthropy, etc.). Advisor value proposition shifts to quarterbacking the relationship and leveraging resources.	Advisors need to be able to distinguish among the various model providers, and effectively evaluate how they are constructed. Advisors may need to use multiple models to solve for their client needs.
Investor	Investors receive access to more specialized expertise and a team working on their behalf. Models let the advisor broaden the set of capabilities that they can deliver to their HNW clients.	The models still need to deliver the results, and advisors need to manage the managers to ensure they fulfill client goals.

For advisors who mainly have transactional, mutual fund wrap, separately managed (SMA), or unified managed accounts (UMA), we discuss the benefits of migrating to model portfolios in Table 5.3.

Models may not be appropriate for every advisor or every client, but they represent an evolutionary step forward for our industry. Asset managers can leverage their asset allocation and portfolio construction expertise, advisors can spend more time and energy addressing wealth management issues, and investors gain a broader team of experts working on their behalf. As with many shifts over the last couple of decades, some advisors may fret that these changes represent a threat to their business models, and others will embrace these changes and evolve their practices. Some advisors will become commoditized, and others will flourish as they pivot to focus on broader wealth management issues.

With the anticipated growth of asset allocation model portfolios, advisors need to be able to effectively evaluate and compare the various providers in the marketplace. The growth of asset allocation

TABLE 5.3 **Benefits of Transitioning to Models**

	Benefits of Transitioning to Models
Transactional	Transaction costs are nearing zero. Consequently, investors see little or no value in this type of relationship. Advisors need to shift their value proposition to focus on how they can help with a broadening set of wealth management issues.
Mutual Fund Wrap	Mutual fund wrap models may be limited by the number and quality of underlying mutual funds. Also, because mutual fund costs are typically higher, the overall expense may be substantially higher than for models that primarily use ETFs.
Traditional SMA Wrap	SMAs may be limited in minimums and ability to adequately diversify exposure across multiple managers. SMA costs are typically higher than those of ETFs; therefore, traditional SMA models may be more expensive than models that include ETFs.
UMA Model	UMA models were built to address some of the limitations of mutual fund wrap models and traditional SMA wrap accounts. UMA models are typically managed by home offices. Leveraging third-party models provides additional objectivity and makes it easier to shift from one model to the next.

models is a good thing for our industry and represents the natural evolution of advisors adapting their business models and value proposition. SMAs did not negate the value of advisors. Rather, they shifted the value proposition to selecting the right combination of SMAs to meet client goals and objectives. The same is true for the growth of models. The advisor's value proposition shifts from building models to selecting third-party models to fulfill client goals.

With robust raw materials, models can provide broad diversification to virtually all market segments, providing global macro exposure or generating income through retirement. Models can be geared toward maximizing returns in rising markets or dampening volatility in choppy markets. Because of models' diverse nature, advisors may choose to use multiple models, depending on client needs. To illustrate model diversity, Table 5.4 provides a sample asset allocation using active and passive strategies.

In the most efficient asset class, US large cap, there is little evidence of consistent outperformance. I therefore split the allocation between multifactor and cheap beta ETFs, to capture excess returns

TABLE 5.4 **Sample Model Allocation**

Asset Class	Percentage	Strategy / Structure
US Large Cap	25%	Multifactor ETF/Cheap Beta (60/40)
US Small Cap	7%	Active Manager/Cheap Beta (50/50)
International Developed	13%	Active Manager/Factor ETF (50/50)
Emerging Markets	5%	Active Manager/Factor ETF (60/40)
Fixed Income	25%	Active Manager
High Yield	5%	Active Manager
Real Assets	5%	Active Manager
Alternatives	10%	Active Manager
Cash	5%	Money Market

and keep costs low. The multifactor exposure can be accomplished in a single ETF, or the model provider may choose to allocate across one or more factor ETF.

For the small cap, I divide the exposure between active management (alpha) and cheap beta ETFs (reduce costs). For international developed and emerging markets, I use active management and factor ETF(s), with no exposure to cheap beta. Research has shown that factor strategies have outperformed their market-cap benchmarks by a wide margin over time.[5] For broad-based fixed income, high yield, real assets, and alternative investments, I suggest using active management options based on manager skill and some of the inherent challenges of accessing markets through a passive strategy.

Advisors now have a multifaceted toolbox to leverage the resources and expertise of a broad set of proprietary and third-party partner firms. Consequently, the advisors' value is in determining how best to use these models to achieve their clients' goals.

DEVELOPING CUSTOMIZED MODELS

Although the growth of models is a positive development for the industry, many HNW and UHNW investors require more customized solutions that include allocations to alternative invest-ments. Therefore, we need to consider the role that the underlying investments play in building a durable portfolio. Table 5.4 provides a high level overview of how we should break down these invest-ments and use them effectively in portfolios.

For HNW and UHNW families, the question is not active ver-sus passive, or traditional versus alternative investments, but rather how to use all of these investments in the most appropriate ways. As an industry, we need to do a better job of identifying how to use the various building blocks better. Traditional ETFs can provide tax-efficient exposure, and factor ETFs can provide excess returns. Some SMAs have shown skill in outperforming the markets, while others deliver after-tax alpha. Hedge funds can serve multiple roles in a portfolio, from capital appreciation to wealth preservation and providing broader diversification. Private equity offers the poten-tial for higher returns, private credit can be an alternative source of income, and real assets can provide diversification away from tradi-tional investments.

TABLE 5.5 Evaluating the Structure and Role of Investments

Passive investing (ETFs and mutual funds)	**Cheap beta** provides cost-effective, tax-efficient exposure to all market segments. Can be used tactically based on its ease of trading. **Smart beta/Factor investing** provides the ability to exploit known factors in beating the market and incorporating tilts and biases in building portfolios.
Active investing (SMAs and mutual funds)	**Active managers** need to demonstrate their value by outperforming the market and/or delivering better after-tax returns. Active managers can demonstrate their value in challenging market environments where skill is at a premium.
Hedge funds (limited partnerships, liquid alternatives, and registered funds)	**Hedge funds** are multifaceted tools that serve different roles in portfolios. They can be broken down into substrategies: equity hedged, event-driven, relative value, macro, and multistrategy.
Private markets (limited partnerships and registered funds)	**Private markets** have historically been the exclusive domain of large institutions and family offices. Private equity can offer increased returns, private credit offers higher income, and real assets provide diversification.

CASE STUDY: UHNW FAMILY

This case study, based on a UHNW family I worked with at Morgan Stanley, illustrates the use of active and passive strategies in a product-agnostic fashion. I have changed the names and some of the details for confidentiality.

Scott Perry sold his company to a large food services conglomerate and set up a family office. Scott and his wife, Elaine, had personal accounts and a joint account. Each of their three children—Susan, Scott Jr., and Joanie—had individual accounts, as did the six grandchildren. Scott also established a family foundation. The family had several hundred million dollars in total. Scott and Elaine had about $250 million in investable wealth, the foundation had approximately $50 million, the children's portfolios ranged from $10 million to $30 million, and the grandchildren's portfolios ranged from $1 million to $5 million.

TABLE 5.6 Perry Family Portfolios

Accounts	Underlying Investments
Scott & Elaine (all entities)	Scott and Elaine had unlimited access to hedge funds, private equity, and SMAs. Because they generated income from royalties, they had little need for fixed income, had a long time horizon, and had healthy exposure to alternative investments. We occasionally used ETFs for tactical allocations.
Family Foundation	The family foundation had large allocations to hedge funds and private equity, as well as exposure to a broad set of globally diversified separately managed account strategies and an unconstrained fixed income mutual fund (institutional shares).
Children	Susan was interested in understanding her portfolio and had higher allocations to hedge funds and private equity. Scott and Joanie were more risk-averse and had small allocations to hedge funds. They each had exposure to multiple SMAs for global diversification, and institutional mutual funds for diversified fixed income exposure. We occasionally used ETFs tactically in Susan's portfolio, to adjust to changing market conditions.
Grandchildren	The two oldest grandchildren had small exposures to a fund-of-funds, while the other grandchildren were allocated across traditional SMAs, mutual funds, and ETFs. We used ETFs to ensure adequate diversification and used liquid alternatives to mimic hedge funds.

The Perry family had significant wealth and could access the industry's best thinking. We spent a lot of time thinking through the allocation across each entity and then considered how best to access exposure to the various asset classes. Wealth advisors should not assume that ETFs are "retail" products just because they are inexpensive. Institutions and family offices have been using passive investing for decades, and ETFs merely represent a more efficient way of accessing a particular market segment. Factor investing takes passive investing to the next level by capturing known factors in an elegant wrapper. It offers *alpha in a beta wrapper.*

Although SMAs are typically a better vehicle to access the equity markets, fixed income is an institutional market, and there is often a scale imperative that makes an institutional mutual fund a better choice. SMAs buying smaller increments may pay higher prices than an institutional manager who may be able to purchase more bonds at a better price because of their size and ability to negotiate.

Wealth advisors should carefully consider vehicle selection in determining how best to access a particular market segment. It is easy to assume that ETFs and mutual funds are retail investments because of their lower minimums, and hedge funds and private equity are HNW and institutional products. but it is not that simple. There are merits to using ETFs and mutual funds with HNW and UHNW families.

KEY TAKEAWAYS

We should no longer debate the merits of active versus passive investing, but rather determine how to best incorporate both in building better portfolios. The lines between active and passive are blurring, with the introductive of active ETFs and index mutual funds. Smart beta strategies bridge the gap between traditional passive strategies and what active managers attempt to deliver, potentially providing alpha in a beta wrapper.

Asset allocation models represent a natural evolution, providing benefits to advisors and investors and shifting the wealth advisor's value proposition from managing assets to quarterbacking the relationship. Wealth advisors can pivot to focus on providing broader wealth management solutions to HNW clients.

Although asset allocation models provide scale and efficiency to an advisor's practice, many HNW and UHNW families require customized solutions to meet their goals. Fortunately, the industry has evolved, providing better tools for building portfolios. Wealth advisors should carefully consider vehicle selection when allocating assets, rather than falling for the assumption that certain products are retail and others are institutional.

CHAPTER 6

The Role and Use of Alternative Investments

Emphasizing inefficiently priced asset classes with interesting active management opportunities increases the odds of investment success. Intelligent acceptance of illiquidity and a value orientation constitute a sensible, conservative approach to portfolio management.

David F. Swensen
Pioneering Portfolio Management:
An Unconventional Approach to Institutional Investment,
Fully Revised and Updated

As an industry, we do not always make it easy for investors to understand the role of a particular type of investment. Consequently, we sometimes scare investors away from what they should be embracing. The term *alternative investments* is a good example of how industry jargon gets in the way and limits the integration of these strategies into investor portfolios. The name alone conjures up fear and confusion.

Are alternative investments just a fancy name for hedge funds? Are they appropriate only for institutions and very wealthy families? To what are they the alternative? This chapter evaluates alternative investments within a goals-based framework: what are we solving for? We will examine various types of alternative investments and how to use them to build goals-based portfolios.

WHY CONSIDER ALTERNATIVES INVESTMENTS?

We define alternative investments as hedge funds and private markets: private equity, private credit, and real assets. The following driving factors should lead to growth in the use of alternative investment strategies by HNW investors:

Market environment. The next 10 years likely will be vastly different from the past 10 years, with lower traditional equity returns and bond yields, and increasing correlations across investments. The markets will be dealing with the impact of the global pandemic, assets with negative yields across the globe, and increasing global tensions. This environment may be conducive for alternative investments to help dampen volatility, provide alternative sources of income, and potentially deliver better returns than traditional investments.

Product and structure development. Product innovation has allowed managers to offer alternative strategies to investors who previously were unable to invest due to accreditation, access, and minimums. New product structures, and improvements to existing structures, provide more and better choices for HNW investors.

Regulatory changes. Regulatory changes have made it easier for privately offered funds to market themselves. The federal Jumpstart Our Business Startups (JOBS) act allowed for crowdfunding and eased restrictions on marketing hedge funds and private equity to individual investors. Along with the new product innovations, regulatory relief has increased the availability of these investments for Main Street investors.

Alternative investments have long been valuable investment tools for family offices and large institutions, allowing both to allocate effectively across an array of underlying strategies. We often use the terms *alternative investments* and *hedge funds* interchangeably, but alternative investments represent a broad array of underlying strategies, while hedge funds describe the structure. Hedge funds are typically available in a limited partnership structure and consequently are only available to qualified purchasers and accredited investors. HNW investors are classified as accredited investors when their net worth is above $1 million, excluding the value of their primary residences, or their annual income is above $200,000 ($300,000 for a couple), while qualified participants are individuals with at least $5 million in investments.

Large institutions have historically allocated significant percentages of their portfolios to alternative investments because of their attractive returns and diversification benefits. In fact, if we examine the allocations of the National Association of Colleges University Business Officers (NACUBO) in Table 6.1, we notice that the larger the endowment, the higher the allocation to alternative investments. Endowments with more than $1 billion in assets under management have more than half of their worth in alternative investments (58 percent), including dedicated allocations to hedge funds, private equity, private credit, and real assets. We would see a similar situation if we examined family offices and pension plans.

We are not recommending that HNW investors allocate more than half of their investments to alternative investments, but rather showing that the savviest investors are making significant allocations to these unique investments. HNW investors have had limited access to many of these strategies historically, and there may be structural trade-offs in accessing certain of these strategies at lower minimums. HNW investors may require greater liquidity than institutions that invest over a longer period.

TABLE 6.1 **NACUBO: Asset Allocation for Fiscal Year 2018**

Size of Endowment	Domestic Equities	Fixed Income	Non-US Equities	Alternative Strategies	Short-Term Securities/ Cash
More than $1 billion	13%	7%	19%	**58%**	3%
$501 million–$1 billion	22%	10%	22%	**41%**	5%
$101–$500 million	24%	12%	22%	**38%**	4%
$51–$100 million	31%	19%	22%	**22%**	3%
$25–$50 million	39%	22%	18%	**16%**	5%
Under $25 million	45%	24%	15%	**11%**	5%

Average asset allocations as of June 30, 2018. All data are dollar-weighted unless otherwise specified. Due to rounding, details may not sum to 100 percent. Alternative strategies are categorized in the NCSE as follows: private equity (LBOs, mezzanine, M&A funds, and international private equity); marketable alternative strategies (hedge funds, absolute return, market neutral, long/short, 130/30, and event-driven and derivatives); venture capital; private equity real estate (noncampus); energy and natural resources (oil, gas, timber, commodities, and managed futures); and distressed debt. On-campus real estate is included in the short-term securities/cash/other category.

Source: NACUBO

Hedge Funds

After the tech bubble burst, HNW investors clamored for strategies to protect their wealth during market shocks. Not surprisingly, interest in hedge funds grew dramatically through the early 2000s. The results warranted attention, as the broad-based hedge fund index substantially outpaced the global equity index (Figure 6.1). Broadly, hedge funds fared much better than most traditional investments during the global financial crisis, with strategies like global macro and managed futures delivering positive returns, while the MSCI World plummeted dramatically.

Over the last 20 years, broad-based hedge funds, as represented by the Hedge Fund Research index, outperformed a global equity index, especially during periods of substantial drawdowns such as 2000, 2003, 2008, and early 2020 (global pandemic). Hedge funds often earn their stripes during volatile periods, due to their ability to be both long and short and the expanded number of investments at their disposal. They often lag in rising bull markets, such as the bull market from 2009 to 2019.

FIGURE 6.1 **Comparative Performance:**
Hedge Funds vs Global Equities

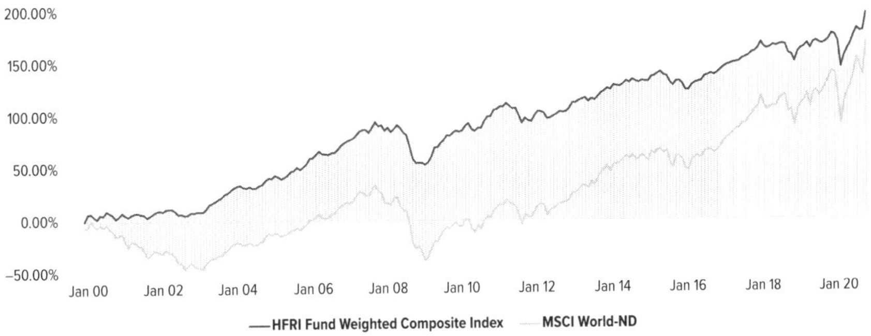

After the global financial crisis of 2008, advisors and HNW investors looked for investments that could help them hedge their market exposure and protect them from big drawdowns. They clamored for hedge fund strategies, but were often limited by the accreditation rules, which restrict investors by wealth and by structural limitations on the number of investors per fund. We will cover these issues later in this chapter. Often the only option available to them was a watered-down mutual fund version of hedge fund strategies (i.e., liquid alternatives), and HNW investors were often disappointed with the results.

Advisors' interest in hedge fund strategies waned through the bull market beginning in 2009, with strong traditional equity returns and the rise of passive investing. After the global financial crisis, the Federal Reserve flooded the markets with liquidity, leading to the longest bull market in history. During this period, the US markets provided returns above their long-term historical averages. Investors could easily access markets through inexpensive ETFs. The flood of passive money drove the markets higher with little regard for valuations and no distinction between a good company with strong fundamentals and a weak company with a flawed business model. Because of the nature of ETFs, the accelerating flow of money into passive investing pushed all companies in an index higher and higher.

The raging bull market made for a difficult environment for many hedge funds. Hedge fund returns often lagged their traditional counterparts and were much more complicated to explain to clients. Wealth advisors could help clients achieve their goals with a combination of active and passive strategies, so they did not need to invest time and effort to understand the nuances of hedge fund strategies. In today's market environment, wealth advisors need to consider expanding their toolbox to include hedge funds.

HEDGE FUND STRATEGIES

Alfred Jones launched the first hedge fund in 1949, using leverage to amplify his long positions and short selling to mitigate market risk. Jones is often referred to as the father of the hedge fund industry, as he was long and short stocks in equal proportion, and his results depended on picking the right stocks to buy and sell. The fund avoided the requirements of the Investment Company Act of 1940 by having no more than 99 investors and using a limited partnership structure. Jones took 20 percent of profits as compensation.

Today, hedge funds retain the core elements of the Jones model: a partnership structure where a percentage of profits is paid as compensation to the fund manager, a finite number of limited partners, and long and short positions used to generate returns. Hedge funds can provide several benefits in a portfolio, including potentially stronger returns, particularly in environments with high volatility and low correlation. They can protect capital, through active risk management and hedging, and can diversify traditional exposures through access to different markets.

Investors often think of hedge funds as being homogenous, when in fact, there is a great deal of diversity from one strategy to the next. Hedge fund strategies represent a broad set of solutions, including equity-hedged, event-driven, relative value, macro, and multi-strategy (see Table 6.2). These can be further broken down into such sub-strategies as market-neutral, activist, fixed income arbitrage, managed futures, and defensive. All hedge fund strategies are not created equal, and not all strategies solve for the same thing. Some provide capital appreciation; others offer wealth preservation and portfolio diversification.

TABLE 6.2 **Breaking Down the Strategies**

Strategy	Substrategy	The Role in Portfolio
Equity-Hedge	Long-short, market-neutral, sector, short-biased, etc.	Capital appreciation
Event-Driven	Activist, merger-arbitrage, distressed, etc.	Capital appreciation
Relative Value	Pairs Trading, Fixed Income Arbitrage, Convertible Arbitrage, etc.	Wealth preservation
Macro	Global macro, managed futures (CTA), currency, etc.	Portfolio diversification
Multistrategy	Equity-hedge, event-driven, relative value, and macro	Portfolio diversification

Equity-hedge. Long-short strategies are long the companies they expect to rise and short those they expect to fall. They attempt to make money by employing either fundamental or quantitative analysis. Shorting a stock requires borrowing stock and then buying it back later before returning it to the lender. It sounds simple, but many inexperienced hedge funds struggle to add value by shorting stocks. Market-neutral strategies use offsetting positions to maintain neutrality or to go long and short on individual stocks or sectors while also maintaining market beta.

Event-driven. Many investors think of hedge funds as they are portrayed in Michael Douglas' movie *Wall Street*. The character Gordon Gekko famously said "greed is good" as he sought to take over a target company. Today, activist investors often take large positions and board seats to unlock value in companies. Activism can result in restructuring or selling off unproductive assets. Merger-arbitrage seeks to take advantage of merger activity, typically taking positions in potential targets before the market prices in a transaction.

Relative value. Relative value strategies take advantage of market mispricings, taking long positions in market sectors that appear undervalued, and short positions in sectors that may be overvalued. Relative value is often referred to as "pairs trading" or "reversion to the mean," as managers trade two highly correlated assets.

Macro. Macro strategies typically exhibit low correlation to the overall market. Global macro strategies invest across various market segments to exploit geopolitical risks and/or economic events. Managed futures is a trend-following strategy that uses future positions across a range of assets, commodities, and currencies. Managed futures can blunt the volatility of market shocks, because they have a low to negative correlation to most traditional assets.

Multistrategy. Multistrategy invests across the various hedge fund strategies, often structured as a fund-of-fund where the manager allocates capital across a range of strategies and underlying hedge funds. The managers provide diversified hedge fund exposure and can choose the strategy they think will perform best in a given market environment.

BENEFITS OF HEDGE FUNDS

Hedge funds are often viewed with a certain amount of skepticism. Investors may think of Jim Simons (Renaissance), Ray Dalio

(Bridgewater), Ken Griffith (Citadel), Steve Cohen (Point72), and David Tepper (Appaloosa), all billionaire investors with personalities as large as their portfolios. Some question whether they have an edge in the market, and whether skill, luck, or something else has led to their outsized results.

Today, more than 8,000 hedge funds represent approximately $3 trillion in assets under management. They include behemoths such as Bridgewater Associates (>$130 billion in assets under management) and small start-ups, seasoned traders as well as those just setting up their firms. Hedge funds represent a diverse group of managers and strategies, with varying degrees of success and skill. Table 6.3 describes some of the pros and cons of hedge funds.

TABLE 6.3 Pros and Cons of Hedge Funds

Pros	Cons
Access to some of the top investors in the world. The compensation structure attracts the most talented managers.	The "2 and 20" fee structure takes a significant bite out of investors returns and dramatically reduces their level of participation.
Access to unique investment opportunities, including illiquid investments.	Some funds have "lock-up" provisions that make it difficult for investors to access their money.
Limited partnership structure provides managers with greater latitude in investing.	Lack of transparency is a major concern for investors in a post-Madoff world.
Some strategies may provide noncorrelation returns and diversification benefits.	Not all funds are created equal and it is difficult to conduct due diligence.

Hedge funds' appeal has long been the ability to tap into the best talent and give them more freedom in identifying investment opportunities. The structure means investors must have a long time horizon, since there are limitations on when and how they get their money back. This lets managers focus on investing for the long run rather than being forced to meet redemptions. Hedge fund managers are rewarded handsomely for generating results with the typical "2 & 20" fee structure.

After 2008, investors began to focus on some of hedge funds' limitations: excessive fees, lack of liquidity, and lack of transparency. The fees are designed to reward the hedge fund. That's fine when they deliver results, but in 2008 many hedge funds lost money and still received fat fees. After the global financial crisis, many investors wanted their money back, only to realize that many hedge funds decided to put up "gates" preventing redemptions. Little-known provisions buried in most offering memorandums gave hedge funds the ability to stop redemptions if they decided that redemptions were harming other investors. As much as 25 percent of all hedge fund assets were gated at the end of 2008.

The other common drawback of hedge funds is the lack of transparency. Unlike mutual funds, SMAs, or ETFs, hedge funds are not required to disclose their holdings. In fact, hedge funds would often like to conceal their positions. For example, when the market becomes aware that an activist hedge fund has taken a large position in a public company, speculation that the activist will push for a change of leadership, an acquisition, or selling off unproductive assets often spikes the stock price.

Bernie Madoff ran an elaborate Ponzi scheme for many years. He created fictitious statements and convinced investors that he was making them money year-over-year. A close cadre of enablers perpetrated this fraud over decades. Prosecutors estimated that this fraud cost investors nearly $65 billion across almost 5,000 accounts. Although Madoff was not running a hedge fund per se, the scandal created a lot of investor concern. Were other hedge funds operating Ponzi schemes? Would investors be able to access their money if necessary? How can we know what a hedge fund is doing?

In many respects, the Madoff scandal ushered in the growth of liquid alternative strategies: hedge funds in a mutual fund structure. Liquid alternatives address some of the structural challenges raised earlier, but at what price? Do liquid alternatives hold the same positions as their hedge fund siblings?

EVALUATING THE STRUCTURES

Product innovation has helped *democratize* alternative investments, making these once allusive strategies available to more investors, in a more liquid and transparent structure. Many asset managers rushed to bring liquid alternatives to the market after 2008. Unfortunately, many of them lacked the requisite experience and infrastructure. Managing long/short portfolios is more complicated than merely picking winners and losers. Trading is different from investing, and entering and exiting positions efficiently can be the difference between successful funds and those that fail. Because these vehicles offered daily liquidity and limited leverage, they were limited in their ability to add alpha over time.

Liquid alternatives have limitations and structural trade-offs, but if they can provide similar diversification benefits, they can be valuable tools for advisors. Registered investment companies (RICs) have emerged as a bridge between hedge funds and traditional mutual funds. Table 6.4 compares the structural trade-offs of liquid alternatives, RICs, and hedge funds.

TABLE 6.4 Structural Considerations

Characteristic	Mutual Funds (liquid alternatives)	Registered Investment Companies (RIC)	Hedge Funds and Funds-of-funds (LP)
Investor Type	All	Varies	Accredited Investor/ Qualified Purchaser
Minimums	Low	Medium	High
Pricing	Daily	Monthly	Monthly
Liquidity	Daily	Monthly or Quarterly	Quarterly or Longer
Lock-up	No	Varies	Yes
Performance Fee	No	Varies	Yes
Transparency	High	High	Low
Tax Reporting	1099	1099 or K-1	K-1
Leverage	Limited	Unlimited	Unlimited

Mutual funds are available to all investors. They offer low minimum investments, daily liquidity, transparency, and 1099 tax reporting. However, to meet liquidity requirements, they may need to hold more liquid securities and limit their leverage. These limitations may mean that they underperform relative to an unconstrained hedge fund.

Registered funds combine many of the benefits of liquid alternatives while still retaining some of the advantages of a hedge fund. Registered funds are available to more investors at lower minimums. They provide increased liquidity with better transparency than hedge funds. Registered funds can use leverage, invest in illiquid investments, and typically provide 1099 tax reporting, which is preferable for investors. RICs must be registered with the Securities and Exchange Commission and must comply with applicable laws.

Hedge funds are only available to accredited investors and qualified purchasers, with high minimums and limited liquidity. They charge performance fees, have lock-up provisions, and provide K-1 tax reporting. Hedge funds can invest in illiquid securities, use leverage generously, and provide limited transparency, which ultimately gives them their investing edge and provides the opportunity to generate alpha.

RISK FACTORS

Advisors and HNW investors need to evaluate structural trade-offs and additional risk factors, including transparency, leverage, and complexity, before investing. Hedge funds may be hesitant to provide full transparency, but ideally they provide access to due diligence professionals who can assure investors that hedge funds are adhering to their stated discipline and not using excess levels of leverage. Advisors and HNW investors should not invest in a hedge fund unless someone has carefully vetted the fund.

Advisors need to compare a hedge fund's fees and liquidity to those of registered funds and liquid alternatives. Fees and limited liquidity may be layered. Understanding several key terms can help investors make an informed decision before allocating to hedge funds:

- **Management fee.** Typically, management fees are 1 to 2 percent per year, charged on a quarterly basis.
- **Performance fee.** 20 percent is the norm, charged at the end of each fiscal year.
- **High-water mark.** The investor only pays the performance fee for any profits earned between its point of entry and its highest level.
- **Lock-up.** Some funds require investors to maintain their capital for a minimum period of time, often 12 months. Some funds use a "soft lock" that serves the same purpose, but with the option for investors to redeem during the lock-up period in exchange for an early withdrawal fee.
- **Redemption frequency.** The majority of funds offer quarterly liquidity. Some now offer monthly liquidity, while others only allow annual redemptions.
- **Notice period.** Investors must notify fund managers about their intention to redeem, usually 30 to 90 days in advance of the redemption date.

THE ROLE OF HEDGE FUNDS

Hedge funds dampen portfolio volatility by accessing different segments of the marketplace and by exercising their freedom to be long and short the market. Historically, this broader investing palette has led to lower correlation to traditional investments and better downside protection.

As the name suggests, hedge funds can play a valuable role in limiting the effect of big drawdowns by *hedging* market exposure. Figure 6.2 shows select asset class returns for 2008. Managed futures and global macro delivered positive results, and the other hedge fund strategies lost less than the S&P 500 (–37%).

FIGURE 6.2 Select Asset Class Returns: 2008

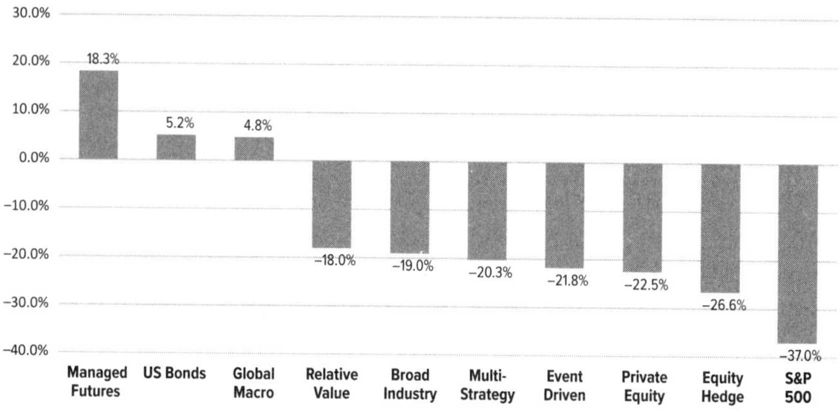

Source: Morningstar Direct

Hedge funds generally flourish in markets with increased volatility and strong distinctions between winning and losing companies. That was not the environment of the bull market from 2009 to 2019, when the markets soared to new highs with record flows into ETFs. The next decade will likely be a very different environment, as global economies deal with the effects of the global pandemic, rising tensions here and abroad, and geopolitical risks.

With a backdrop of increased volatility and more shocks to global markets, hedge funds will likely be able to earn their stripes by taking advantage of market dislocations in the coming years. The next decade will be an environment in which the skilled hedge fund manager can add considerable value relative to traditional investments. Traditional returns will likely be muted and well below historical norms, while hedge funds will have greater flexibility in exploiting opportunities across the various market segments.

Hedge funds can also be an alternative source of income for HNW investors. With traditional fixed income at generationally low levels, and $12 trillion of negative-yielding assets globally, hedge funds have greater flexibility in the types of securities they can invest in, including high yield, distressed debt, leveraged loans, collateralized loan obligations, credit card receivables, public and private real estate, and royalties. Alternative credit strategies have become increasingly popular as HNW investors recognize the challenge of generating yield in today's market environment.

Hedge funds provide an opportunity for better returns and higher income than traditional investments and may offer better downside protection. It is still important to choose which type of strategy fulfills various roles in a portfolio. Equity-hedge and event-driven strategies are more focused on capital appreciation, relative value provides wealth preservation, and macro and multistrategy provide portfolio diversification.

EVALUATING HEDGE FUNDS

Divide hedge fund due diligence into investment due diligence and operational due diligence. Investment due diligence focuses on team experience, historical track record, fund size, leverage use, and risk management controls. Operational due diligence focuses on trading controls, compliance, cybersecurity, pricing, and service providers such as auditors. Advisors may choose to leverage due diligence conducted by their firm or outside providers, but should ensure that hedge funds have been carefully vetted before recommending them to clients.

Advisors should review documentation describing the fund, including fact sheets, offering memorandums and research/due diligence reports. Advisors should pay careful attention to the following risk factors:

- **Transparency.** Depending on the structure, hedge funds have varying levels of transparency. As much as is practical, advisors should try to ascertain whether managers are adhering to their stated disciplines.
- **Liquidity.** Carefully review liquidity provisions in advance. How liquid is the structure? What is the notice period?
- **Complexity.** Understand the strategy employed. If it sounds too complicated or too good to be true, it may make sense to pass on the investment.
- **Time horizon.** Before you invest, understand how long it may take for a particular strategy to play out and determine which market environment rewards a particular type of strategy.
- **Leverage.** Understand how much leverage a fund uses and how that compares to similar funds. Leverage tends to magnify portfolio results, both up and down.

Mark Felt, associate director of the Federal Bureau of Investigation, was known as "Deep Throat" when he served as a confidential source during the Watergate investigation. "Follow the money," he famously told *Washington Post* reporters Bob Woodward and Carl Bernstein. Woodward and Bernstein followed the money, eventually leading to President Nixon's impeachment. Advisors should follow Felt's advice and follow the money in evaluating alternative investment strategies. Carefully examine the fee structure and any related payments. Depending on the structure, a hedge fund may charge multiple layers of fees. Hedge funds may also pay to be included on a firm's platform. Dig a little deeper to understand the economics of these unique strategies.

As previously mentioned, I worked at Morgan Stanley from 1995 to 2008 and often received inquiries from UHNW families about investing with Bernie Madoff. At the time, Madoff had developed a cultlike following, based largely on his claims that he generated remarkably consistent results over time—never losing money— and his reputation as former chairman of NASDAQ and various philanthropic efforts. Madoff was charismatic and active in Jewish communities in New York and Florida. Madoff often claimed that he was closed to new investors, but would make exceptions for wealthy families and institutions. In reality, he needed new investors to perpetuate his Ponzi scheme. Madoff claimed to employ a "split-strike" conversion strategy.

Not surprisingly, Madoff was very secretive about his strategy and was unwilling to allow many firms on-site to conduct due diligence. For those allowed on-site, he fabricated statements showing transactions that generated the results and could point to an outside audit verifying the results. However, if you compared the transactions to the tape, you would have realized they were false, and if you visited the accounting firm, you would have realized it was a one-man shop with one client—not one of the big accounting firms that you would expect for a firm of Madoff's size.

Famed whistleblower Harry Markopolis had given the SEC a detailed road map chronicling Madoff's fraud. In his Senate testimony, Markopolis described his numerous attempts to expose the Madoff fraud, beginning in 2000 and with subsequent submissions to the SEC in 2001, 2005, 2007, and 2008. Markopolis challenged any manager's ability to deliver such consistent results: 10 to 20 percent per annum, with no losses. He questioned how Madoff could have made his supposed trades, which would have exceeded the stated daily volume, and questioned Madoff's cozy relationship with the small accounting firm auditing his results.

What Can We Learn from the Madoff Scandal?

1. If it sounds too good to be true, it probably is. Do not invest unless you understand how a strategy works.
2. Compare results with those of similar strategies.

3. Do not confuse marketing with due diligence.
4. Beware the "exclusivity" pitch.
5. Numbers can be misleading. Dig deeper.
6. Evaluate compliance controls and independence.
7. Evaluate the accounting firm. (Hedge funds generally use the top firms.)
8. Evaluate the pricing services.
9. Review independent custodians/brokerage statements.
10. Make sure that firms are registered with the appropriate regulator.

I would never invest in an alternative investment, or any complex strategy, without having a reputable firm conduct advance due diligence. Investors should always know *what* they own and *why* they own it. If you don't understand a particular strategy, and don't know what role it plays in your portfolio, it may make sense to pass on the opportunity. You may miss out on an exciting opportunity or you may avoid a colossal mistake, but at least you'll understand the overall strategy in place.

A GOALS-BASED FRAMEWORK

Goals-based investing has become increasingly popular over the past several years because it tracks progress relative to a goal rather than to an arbitrary benchmark. Investors often fall into the trap of using three benchmarks to measure success: the S&P 500, cash, and their best friend's portfolio—whichever performed best. Investors gripe if their diversified portfolios underperform the S&P 500 in a rising market, or complain that they would be better served sitting in cash during market corrections. Too often they focus on how well they performed relative to a friend or family member.

These comparisons are rarely appropriate. We would all benefit from moving away from fixating on short-term benchmarks and instead focus on progress relative to personal goals. There is value in changing the discussion with investors to the role of various asset classes individually, and then focusing on how those classes fit within an overall portfolio. Think of the underlying investments as puzzle pieces that you can assemble to see a more complete picture.

Not all hedge fund strategies solve for the same thing, so think of hedge funds as discrete solutions. Like your equity allocation, equity-hedge and event-driven strategies are designed to provide capital preservation in a portfolio. Like your fixed-income allocation, a relative value strategy is designed to provide wealth preservation (stability) in a portfolio. Like your allocation to cash and gold, macro and multistrategies are designed to provide portfolio diversification and downside protection (defense).

By switching the discussion to a goals-based framework and focusing on what the underlying strategies are designed to provide, we can more effectively measure their value in a portfolio. Hedge funds are valuable tools that advisors and HNW investors should embrace. Compared with such traditional tools as hammers, nails, and saws, hedge funds are power tools: power drills, table saws, and nail guns. They are more sophisticated and multifaceted, able to use a broader set of securities and be long and short the market. With the proliferation of better tools for building portfolios, we need to better understand how to use them appropriately.

Hedge funds are versatile tools for building better portfolios, but they are often misunderstood and so investors shy away from them. Hedge funds provide valuable diversification relative to traditional investments, and in periods of market stress, they may help mitigate big drawdowns. The next decade will likely see lower traditional returns, increased market shocks, and a more pronounced distinction between winners and losers. This is an environment where hedge funds should flourish. Advisors should use these valuable tools to help their clients achieve their long-term goals.

CHAPTER 7

Innovations in Private Markets

It's clear to me when you do private equity well, you're making companies more efficient and helping them grow and become more profitable. That success means our investors—such as public pension funds—benefit, which contributes to the economic wealth of society.

David Rubenstein
Cofounder, the Carlyle Group

PRIVATE EQUITY HAS LONG BEEN A UNIQUE AND ELUSIVE INVEST-ment that was available only to large endowments, foundations, pension plans, and family offices. In recent years, private equity has become more accessible to a broader group of investors, often at lower minimums, because of such factors as product innovation, regulatory developments, and the growing number of private companies.

Investors often think about private equity when a company goes public via an IPO or when a company is bought by a private equity firm, then improved and resold to a corporate buyer. In many respects, the IPO is the culmination of the American dream: taking an idea and turning it into a viable company, and then reaping the rewards. The headlines focus on the tremendous wealth founders and early investors earn as they ring the opening bell. This journey likely would not be possible without the capital, experience, and guidance provided by private equity firms.

In this chapter, we explore the growth and opportunities in private markets: private equity, private credit, and real assets. We examine growth drivers and consider their sustainability, explore how advisors and investors can access this once-elusive asset class, and consider some of the structural trade-offs.

Before investing in private equity, advisors and investors must understand the various stages of development and the corresponding associated risk, from venture capital through growth to buyout opportunities. As private equity has become more available to a larger group of investors, advisors need to get up to speed about product innovation and the options available to their clients. The most common questions I hear from advisors are "How can I evaluate the various private market options?" and "How much should I allocate to private markets?" We will cover these questions in this chapter.

WHY PRIVATE MARKETS—WHY NOW?

As we have previously covered, capital market assumptions for traditional investments are projected to be substantially lower than their historical averages over the next 10 to 15 years. The traditional 60/40 portfolio will likely fall well short of the long-term historical averages. Private equity provides an opportunity for higher returns, private credit provides alternative sources of income, and real assets offer broader diversification. Advisors should consider a broader set of asset classes to achieve their client's goals.

Private equity is projected to deliver returns of approximately 9–10 percent over the next 10 years, a roughly 3 percent illiquidity premium over traditional equity returns. This is due to multiple factors, including the growing number of private companies and the falling numbers of public companies. Today, there are approximately 3,700 public companies, nearly half the number that existed 20 years ago. Many companies are staying private longer and some choose not to go public at all.

The private market universe, by comparison, is quite large and growing, encompassing roughly 98 percent of the largest 185,000 companies. More than 20,000 private companies have more than $100 million in annual revenues—just 3,000 public companies have comparable revenues. Public companies are also getting older, with an average age of more than 20 years. That average was 12 years in 2017. Age matters because company growth typically slows as firms mature.

David Swensen, CIO of the Yale Endowment, is often cited as the savviest investor of this generation. He has espoused the virtues of alternative investments, which have led to Yale's stellar growth over the past couple of decades. Although the Yale Endowment is quite different from the average HNW investor, it is instructive to review its 2021 target allocation (Figure 7.1), especially its large allocations to absolute return (hedge funds), venture capital and leveraged buyouts (private equity), and real estate and natural resources (real assets), as well as its low allocation to traditional investments (foreign and domestic equity, bonds, and cash).

The university's long-term results put it in the top tier of institutional investors. "The endowment returned 10.9 percent annualized over the 10-year period ending June 30, 2020. Yale's 20-year asset class performance remains strong. Domestic equities returned 9.7 percent, besting the benchmark by 3.5 percent annually. Foreign equities produced returns of 14.8 percent, surpassing the composite benchmark by 9.3 percent annually. Absolute return produced an annualized return of 8.1 percent. Leveraged buyouts returned 11.2 percent, while venture capital returned 11.6 percent. Real estate and natural resources contributed annual returns of 8.3 percent and 13.6 percent, respectively."[1]

Consider the differences between individual investors and institutions, as well as Yale's scale imperative. Yale is an endowment,

FIGURE 7.1 Yale Endowment Target Allocation

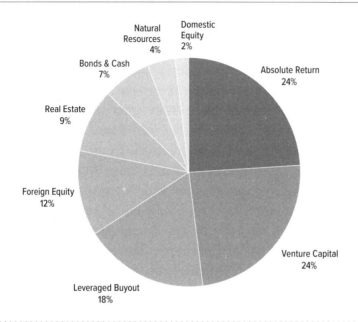

Source: *Yale News*, September 24, 2020

and its time horizon is perpetuity. Individual investors often have cash-flow needs and may not be willing or able to lock up funds for many years. Yale has student payments and alumni donations as additional funding sources. Most of us would hesitate to ask friends or family for financial support due to performance shortfalls.

Yale has a scale imperative relative to an individual investor. Yale can negotiate favorable terms with hedge fund managers and access unique private market opportunities that aren't available to the typical HNW investor. Yale can seed new managers and demand "favored nation status." Yale also employs a deep, dedicated team of professionals to analyze strategies. Most wealth management firms and family offices have dedicated teams to source and conduct due diligence. Most HNW investors lack the expertise and resources to evaluate these strategies on their own.

I would never suggest blindly following the endowment model, but I do believe we can learn valuable lessons by studying the best and brightest investors. Private markets can provide a source of incremental returns, an alternative source of income, and diversification from traditional investments.

Until recently, HNW investors have had limited access to private markets. However, product innovation, changing accreditation standards, and more willingness on the part of private equity firms to bring products to market have changed the investing landscape. This once-elusive asset class can now be accessed by a broader group of investors, at lower minimums, with greater liquidity than ever before.

WHAT IS PRIVATE EQUITY'S APPEAL?

Private equity has historically delivered strong absolute and relative returns compared to traditional public market indices (Figure 7.2). Over the past 20 years, private equity returns have outpaced those of broad-based indices such as the S&P 500 and Russell 2000 (9.6 percent versus 5.3 percent and 6.1 percent, respectively). We will explore how private equity has been able to deliver these strong results and discuss whether these returns will continue.

Private equity's appeal is the opportunity to invest in early-stage companies and reap the benefits as companies go public. Investors get in on the ground floor of the next Google, Facebook, Tesla, or Airbnb. However, private equity represents a range of opportunities across various stages of development. On one end of the spectrum, we find venture capital: early-stage companies that are still developing their product or service. At the other end of the spectrum, we find buyout: cash-flow-positive companies that may benefit from reorganizing or selling certain assets.

Depending on a company's developmental stage, private equity managers can help in different ways, from launching new products

FIGURE 7.2 **Select Asset Class Returns**

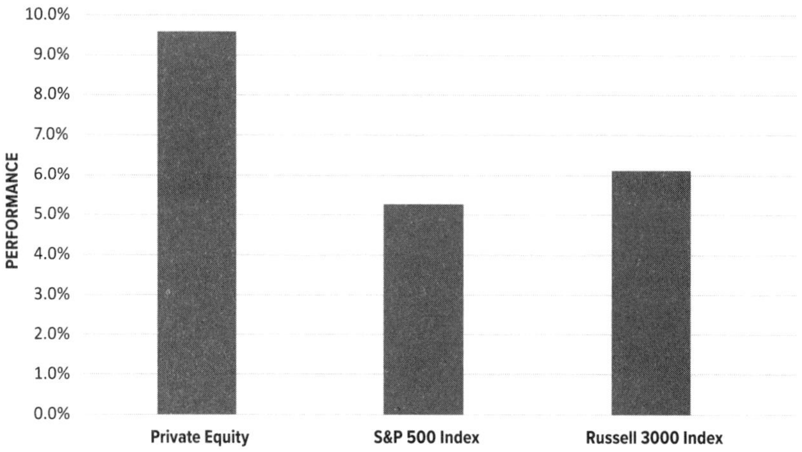

Source: Hamilton Lane Data via Cobalt and eVestment. Data is from Q2 2000–Q2 2020

and services to spinning off noncore businesses or making strategic acquisitions. They can drive value creation by adding leadership, expanding a company's geographic footprint, negotiating favorable terms, and/or spending on marketing. Private equity managers can add value through bolt-on transactions or by consolidating businesses. Let's explore three of these stages in greater detail (Figure 7.3).

Venture companies are at an early stage of an idea for a unique product, service, or technology. Early-stage venture may have little to no revenue and needs capital to bring its ideas to life. Founders often seek capital to fund their business plans. Google, Facebook, and Uber began as fledgling companies with ideas that would change the market. They needed capital early on to fund those ideas. When they ultimately went public, they made substantial money for their founders and early investors.

Growth companies have a proven business model, are growing rapidly, and are either profitable or have a clear path to profitability, with revenues growing 20 percent or more annually. Private equity firms typically take a minority stake in the company and work with the management team to help create value through operational improvements and revenue growth, either organic or through acquisition.

Buyout companies have stable revenues and cash flow. A private equity fund purchases firms at this stage through a leveraged buyout and executes a long-term value creation plan, which may involve organic growth, inorganic growth, and operational improvements, before selling the company. These represent the largest segment of private capital.

FIGURE 7.3 **Stages of Private Equity**

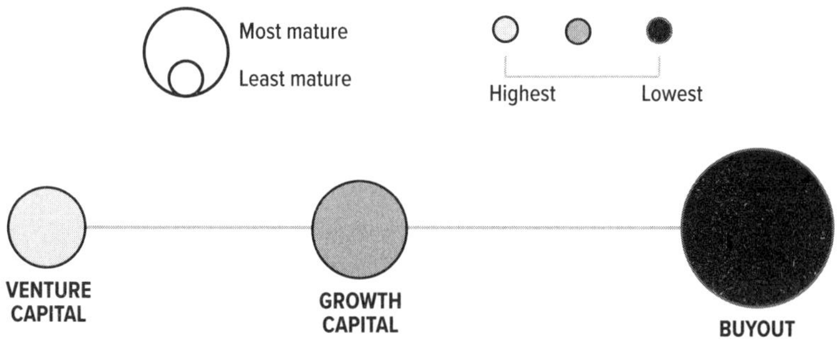

VALUE CREATION

Private companies have the luxury of planning for the long run. Public companies, by contrast, often suffer from a short-term perspective, struggling to meet quarterly market expectations. In a *Wall Street Journal* op-ed, Warren Buffet and Jamie Dimon noted that, "Companies frequently hold back on technology spending, hiring, and research and development to meet quarterly earnings forecasts that may be affected by factors outside the company's control, such as commodity-price fluctuations, stock-market volatility and even the weather."[2]

By contrast, private companies can focus on executing long-term strategies without having to appease shareholders. The results show that this freedom is a substantial benefit. Private equity managers focus on creating value over three to six years. They often bring operating expertise and can help founders develop and implement a multiyear plan, which often leads to stronger growth than public companies enjoy.

Private companies also benefit from an information advantage. Public companies are required to disclose financial information and key business drivers to shareholders. Most public companies are also widely scrutinized by Wall Street research, so all information is priced into the stock price. Conversely, the private markets are inefficient, and skilled private equity managers can exploit their informational advantage to identify attractive acquisitions. Once an acquisition happens, private equity managers can focus on executing their long-term strategy without the distraction of public scrutiny.

Although we often focus on the value of infusing financial capital into a young or struggling company, there is also tremendous value in adding human capital: seasoned managers who have operating experience, industry knowledge, and vast networks. According to a 2020 McKinsey Report, *A New Decade for Private Markets*,[3] every one of the largest 25 private equity firms has significant internal operating groups. These firms focus on attracting and retaining operating talent who can bring their expertise to private companies.

THE LIFE CYCLE OF PRIVATE EQUITY FUNDS

Private equity funds are long-term investments (7 to 10 years), because of the way they deploy capital and their timing for generating returns. Figure 7.4 illustrates the stages of private equity and

FIGURE 7.4 Life Cycle of Private Equity Funds

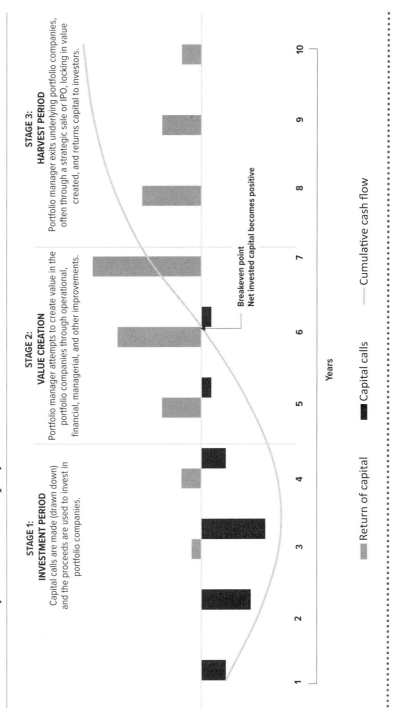

STAGE 1:
INVESTMENT PERIOD
Capital calls are made (drawn down) and the proceeds are used to invest in portfolio companies.

STAGE 2:
VALUE CREATION
Portfolio manager attempts to create value in the portfolio companies through operational, financial, managerial, and other improvements.

STAGE 3:
HARVEST PERIOD
Portfolio manager exits underlying portfolio companies, often through a strategic sale or IPO, locking in value created, and returns capital to investors.

Breakeven point
Net invested capital becomes positive

Years

Return of capital   Capital calls   Cumulative cash flow

the corresponding cash flows. During the investment period, the company draws down capital as it sources investment opportunities. During the value creation stage, private equity managers improve target companies' operational efficiency. During the harvest period, private equity managers exit the underlying investments through a sale or initial public offering.

The line in this table illustrates the cash flow associated with a typical private equity investment. This is often referred to as the J-curve, with drawdown in the early stage of private equity investing and sharp reversal as the firm unlocks value in the underlying investment.

Private equity firms provide critical capital to early-stage companies. They often raise multiple rounds of capital. Company valuations can change continually. As said earlier, private equity managers bring operational expertise and strategic leadership to private companies. Founders often lack the expertise to manage a company through the growth phase or to bring a company public, if that's the desired path. We can all think of multiple great founders who were subpar business managers. Private equity replaces some of those managers as companies mature, and surrounds others with experienced business managers before the firm goes public.

PRIVATE CREDIT

With global yields at historically low levels, investors are increasingly seeking alternative yield sources, and private credit has become an attractive source of return. Private credit has historically offered attractive risk-adjusted results. Direct lending has been the fastest-growing segment of this market.

Investing in the debt of private companies is another way investors can gain exposure to private companies, potentially with less risk involved than a private equity company. Like public company debt, private credit may offer investors an attractive income stream.

Typically, private credit has low correlation to other, more traditional fixed income, because the debt is not traded and subject to the volatility of the public markets. The debt is often at floating interest rates, so investor income rises with overall interest rates—an attractive feature in a rising rate environment.

Funds dedicated to private credit have grown substantially since the GFC, because both institutional investors and retail investors are seeking attractive levels of yield in a low-rate environment. The growth of these funds is partially attributable to a decline in lending by banks in the aftermath of the global financial crisis and because of the Dodd-Frank Wall Street Reform and Consumer Protection Act of 2010.

According to the 2020 Preqin Global Private Debt Report,[4] private credit soared to $812 billion as of June 2019. Assets under management have grown consistently each year, and private credit now has surpassed infrastructure and natural resources to become the third-largest private market asset class.

The market has expanded continuously ever since the GFC, when banks retrenched from serving the middle market as they derisked their balance sheets. Private credit firms swooped in to capitalize on the void. Demand has given rise to a record number of fund managers (1,764)—more than twice as many as existed five years ago.

Before investing in private credit, investors must consider the type of debt in which the fund is investing to appropriately assess the fund's risk level relative to the underlying securities. Consider the capital structure hierarchy to determine which type of investment has preference and priority.

Note the type of underlying debt held in portfolios. Senior secured debt has priority over second lien, mezzanine, and equity holders. In other words, senior secured debt holders have a preferential claim on assets if a company becomes financially distressed.

Investors can access private credit investments through a variety of fund structures, all of which have natural trade-offs that investors must assess.

REAL ASSETS

Real assets include real estate, infrastructure, and natural resources. Real estate is the largest segment of real assets, where funds acquire, finance, or own a variety of property types, including residential, commercial, and industrial. There is a big difference between private real estate and publicly traded REITs (real estate investment trusts).

Private real estate funds are typically broken down by their place on the risk-return spectrum. Core funds are the most conservative, and opportunistic funds have the highest risk. Core funds are primarily focused on high-quality real estate assets in major metropolitan areas, with stable occupancy, steady revenues, and little or no management. They typically use the lowest debt and are the most passive. By contrast, opportunistic funds typically invest in stressed or distressed properties that need major renovations and even potential development work.

Natural resources are raw materials that can be used for economic production or consumption. Investments in natural resources include land, timberland, farmland, traditional and renewable energy, and precious metals. Natural resources investments often exhibit low correlation to traditional investments; they may also offer inflation protection. Moreover, areas such as renewable energy are becoming increasingly popular with investors, in line with a heightened interest in sustainability.

Infrastructure is a set of facilities or systems supporting a country, state, city, or other area. Infrastructure investments include roads, bridges, water treatment facilities, ports, utilities, hospitals, and airports. These investments are often sought out because of their relatively low volatility compared to traditional investments and their potential for inflation protection. Plenty of rhetoric over the past several years has been about the need to rebuild our decaying infrastructure. Perhaps this will be an area of growth in the coming years, fueling economic expansion and paving the way for a modern transportation network.

PRODUCT EVOLUTION

As we've covered, because the primary users of alternative investments were initially institutions and family offices, they were structured to support the needs of long-term investors with significant capital that could be tied up for an extended period of time. But as more HNW investors began to demand access to alternative investments, the structures needed to evolve to meet the needs of this important segment.

Product innovation has sought to address some of the limitations of the classic private equity structures: minimums, tax reporting, and liquidity. Feeder funds, interval funds, and tender offer funds have helped democratize private market investing and address some of the structural limitations (see Table 7.1).

TABLE 7.1 **Evolution of Private Fund Structures**

	Classic LPs	Feeder Funds	Interval Funds	Tender Offer Funds
Minimums	High ($5M)	Lower ($150K–$250K)	Lower ($25K)	Lower ($25K)
Accreditation	Qualified purchaser only	Qualified purchaser only	Accredited investor or lower	Accredited investor
Tax Reporting	K-1	K-1	1099	1099
Liquidity	Limited	Limited	Limited	Limited

Classic LP funds are available only to qualified purchasers, typically at higher minimums and limited liquidity. Because these investments are structured as limited partnerships, investors receive K-1 tax reporting, which is often delayed and may be prone to restatements. Investors commit capital that is drawn down over time (capital calls).

Feeder funds have become popular with HNW investors because they let investors pool capital and access top-tier funds at lower minimums. The feeder fund gives general partners scale and efficiency. Feeder funds are available to qualified participants, who are then subject to capital calls. There is no cash drag, because feeder funds aren't required to meet short-term liquidity demands.

Interval funds are available to accredited investors or even to those with lower accreditation at lower minimums and quarterly liquidity. Interval funds are typically private credit funds. They are not subject to capital calls and provide reporting via 1099 forms. To meet liquidity demands, interval funds may experience cash drag: the cost of being liquid enough to meet redemption requirements.

Tender funds are available to accredited investors at lower minimums, with liquidity via a tender offer. The board decides how much liquidity they'll provide and when. Tender offer funds typically hold private equity. They are not subject to capital calls and provide 1099 tax reporting. Tender offer funds are not required to hold liquid assets.

As noted, structural trade-offs may allow for greater flexibility in how advisors allocate to private markets. Feeder funds provide scale and efficiency, but are only available to qualified participants. Interval funds offer greater liquidity and better tax reporting, but often experience a significant cash drag and may not have access to the best opportunities. Tender offer funds are available to a broader group of investors at lower minimums and better liquidity, but may not own the best private companies.

If investors have the wherewithal, they may be better served by broad-based diversification across private equity. Diversification can broaden investment opportunities, lower risk, and minimize cash drag. Advisors should consider diversification across manager, stage, industry, and vintage. Private markets offer attractive investment opportunities, especially because product innovation has helped democratize these valuable asset classes.

Product structures like "auction funds" sound appealing, but the jury is still out regarding how well this new structure will work when investors try to redeem shares. Auction funds are structured as continuously offered, closed-end funds. They are designed to address the cash drag associated with other structures by providing an auction process that works like an ETF.[5]

With new products coming to the market, and established managers addressing the demand of HNW investors, this once-elusive asset class is becoming a more viable investment option for a growing number of investors.

RISK CONSIDERATIONS

Private markets provide the opportunity for strong returns and diversification relative to traditional investments, but advisors and investors should also evaluate the risks associated with these markets before investing. Risks include a lack of transparency compared to the public markets, with investments typically valued on a quarterly basis. Private market investments are also typically illiquid, and investors should be prepared to stay invested in a private market funds for the entirety of its term of 7 to 10 years.

Private market investors may also be subject to concentration risk. Private market holdings may be concentrated in a few funds, so they may carry a higher likelihood of loss of capital than a more diversified portfolio would. Advisors should educate their clients about the long-term nature of the private markets, with capital distributions typically beginning in the third or fourth year of a fund's life. Other considerations include leverage, as well as the inherent complexity of the asset class's structure. Many private equity funds, especially leveraged buyouts, use leverage as part of their transaction structures, as well as often taking on fund-level leverage, which comes with additional inherent risk.

Depending on the structure, there may be additional risks to consider. For example, more liquid structures may come at a price:

a significant cash drag. Fees may also vary significantly from one structure to the next, and managers may be incented to put their best ideas in the less-liquid, higher-margin structure to avoid a forced liquidation.

INCORPORATING PRIVATE MARKETS

Consider several asset allocation and portfolio construction issues before allocating to private markets. Advisors and investors should evaluate:

- **Risk and return.** What are the expectations and assumptions?
- **Liquidity.** Are there limitations on how long capital may be locked up?
- **Time horizon.** What is the overall portfolio's time horizon?
- **Diversification.** Can you diversify across manager, stage, region, industry, and vintage?
- **Asset location.** What is the appropriate entity / account type to hold the investment?
- **Target allocation.** What is the appropriate target allocation?

Allocating to private equity, private credit, and real assets requires knowledge, access, and investment acumen. Advisors need to understand how the strategies work and how to incorporate them appropriately. They need access to the best strategies in the most appropriate structures, and they need to understand the role of private markets in building a diversified portfolio. With so much of an advisor's value proposition commoditized through robo financial planning and asset allocation, these unique investments let advisors add considerable value to investors.

Selecting the right private equity fund can provide a large premium. As Figure 7.5 illustrates, the dispersion of return in the top-quartile private equity fund is much larger than in the bottom quartile fund, and substantially larger than that of traditional investments and hedge funds. Therefore, there is big premium in selecting the right private equity fund due to the large interquartile spread between the top and bottom quartile funds.

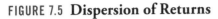

FIGURE 7.5 Dispersion of Returns

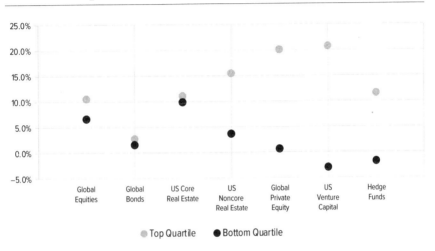

Sources: Lipper, NCREIF, Cambridge Associates, HFRI, J.P. Morgan Asset Management. Global equities (large cap) and global bonds dispersion are based on the world large stock and world bond categories, respectively. Manager dispersion is based on 2Q 2010–2Q 2020 annual returns.

WHAT'S NEXT?

With private markets becoming more accessible and capital market assumptions pointing toward more challenging returns from traditional investments, we will likely see continued interest in this important asset class. The HNW investor demand is leading to more focus on identifying and vetting quality managers and making them available across the various platforms. Recognizing the demand and corresponding opportunity, many asset managers are developing products for HNW investors. Some that lack the necessary expertise may choose to partner with established private equity firms.

There are a couple of trends worth noting as we consider *what's next,* including private equity in retirement plans, impact investing, and the need for better education.

Private Equity in Retirement Plans

In a surprisingly bold move, the US Department of Labor (DOL) and the Securities and Exchange Commission have indicated a willingness to allow private equity in retirement plans. Private equity has long been a significant component of large defined benefit plans, but not available in defined contribution or 401(k) plans. This latest development is motivated by a recognition that private equity offers the potential for higher returns, and consequently would help retirees grow their retirement assets.

The DOL provided additional guidance to consider in allowing private funds in retirement plans:

- The impact of the private equity allocation on diversification, expected return, and fees on a long-term basis
- The ability of plan fiduciaries to oversee private equity investments, versus hiring an expert consultant
- The percent invested in private equity, noting that the SEC limits illiquid assets to 15 percent for registered open-end investment companies
- Whether plan participants will be permitted to take benefit distributions and move into other investment options
- Agreement by plan fiduciaries to value private equity investments according to accounting standards and subject those investments to an annual audit
- Whether the long-term nature and liquidity restrictions of any private equity investments align with plan participants' ability to take distributions or change investment options as they wish
- The adequacy of participant disclosures regarding the character and risks of a plan investment option that includes

a private equity component, to allow participants to make an informed assessment before investing

This development is a significant step forward in bringing the private markets to Main Street. It is a recognition that these investments can help investors grow their retirement nest eggs. There is still work to be done in determining the optimal structure, as liquidity comes at a price and investors need a lot more education about the nuances of private markets.

Impact Investing

One of the biggest trends across the financial services industry has been the growing demand for sustainable investing. As previously noted, sustainable investing can align an investor's purpose and portfolio. Data suggests that investors can *do good* and *do well* at the same time.

The idea that investors can improve society while seeking solid returns is rapidly gaining acceptance. Many private equity funds are incorporating environmental, social, and governance screening into their strategies, and investors' interest in ESG investing has certainly become more commonly accepted. This is a particularly important issue with women and millennials.

The number of fund managers who have signed the UN-supported Principles for Responsible Investment grew to more than 2,000 in 2018, from 1,200 in 2013. The $82 trillion in assets under management by these signatories increased at a compound annual rate of 19 percent in the same period. Of 22,000 investors worldwide, 78 percent said they place more emphasis on sustainability now than they did five years earlier, according to Schroders 2017 Global Investor Study. More than 90 percent of the world's 250 largest companies published corporate social responsibility or sustainability reports in 2018, compared with 45 percent in 2002.

The shift to sustainable investing reflects growing public concern about global challenges such as climate change, plastics pollution, deforestation, social inequality, and access to clean water. Retail investors, especially the millennial generation and women, are increasingly demanding that companies disclose their practices. According to Morgan Stanley's Institute for Sustainable Investing, millennials are twice as likely as the overall population to buy products from sustainable companies. With an estimated $30 trillion of wealth expected to change hands from baby boomers to millennials in the next 30 years, the stakes for investors are significant.

At the other end of the spectrum, family offices and HNW families are often active members of society, charities, and even politics. Many seek to have a positive impact on society through various platforms, including philanthropy. For examples, consider the Gates Foundation (healthcare and fighting poverty), the Rockefeller Foundation (health and science), the Bloomberg Foundation (environment and gun control), the Schwab Foundation (financial literacy), and the Bezos Foundation (education). Impact investing is another venue for family offices and foundations to extend their mission-oriented work.

With the growing demand from client segments large and small, it isn't surprising that a growing number of impact funds are coming to the market. Private equity firms are uniquely positioned to invest in these opportunities, because they are not encumbered by generating short-term profits and they maintain significant control, which lets them drive impact and strong financial results.

Advisor Education

Although the appeal of private markets is apparent, we need substantially more and better education about the proper use of these unique investments. Advisors need to understand the various stages of private equity, growth drivers, the illiquidity premium, and the structural trade-offs. Advisors should also understand how private credit has filled the void created by banks, deploying hundreds of billions of dollars to fund middle market companies. They must be familiar with the risk, return, and correlation benefits of real assets, and how they can be an integral part of a diversified portfolio.

Advanced education can help advisors steer their clients through this new landscape with its unique terminology and vernacular—VC, LBO, J-curve, feeder fund, interval fund, and capital structure hierarchy, to name a few.

Fortunately, organizations such as the CAIA Association, the Investments and Wealth Institute, and the CFA Institute have recognized this challenge and have begun to offer research and education to wealth advisors. Many of the larger asset managers have also developed their own content to address the need for more and better education regarding investing in private markets.

KEY TAKEAWAYS

With traditional investments trending toward lower returns and private markets offering strong absolute and relative returns, institutions and family office investors have been increasing their allocations to private equity, private credit, and real assets. Historically, these investments were not available to many HNW investors, but through product innovation and large private capital firms' willingness to meet industry demand, HNW investors can now access these unique investments at lower minimums.

Advisors should take the lead in educating investors about how to incorporate these strategies. Private markets can play a valuable role in a diversified portfolio, potentially increasing returns, providing alternative income sources, and offering diversification relative to traditional investments. Investors need to understand the risks and structural trade-offs before investing and should view private markets as long-term investments.

CHAPTER 8

Sustainable Investing

A true conservationist is a man who knows that the world is not given by his fathers but borrowed from his children.

John James Audubon

ONE OF THE BIGGEST TRENDS ACROSS THE FINANCIAL SERVICES industry has been the growth of sustainable investing, in both the number of products and the asset growth over the past couple of years. Even with this rapid growth, there is still a false narrative that *doing good* in your portfolio means that you must give up returns, and consequently some advisors and investors have been slow to embrace sustainable investing strategies. Institutional investors in Europe, public funds, endowments, foundations, family offices, women, and millennials have led the adoption of these misunderstood strategies. We have begun to see broader adoption across all client segments in the past couple of years.

Several factors have led to confusion and the initial slow adoption of sustainable investing. The terminology used to describe this approach—socially responsible investing (SRI); environmental, social, and governance (ESG); impact investing; and sustainable investing—is perhaps the biggest area of confusion. The terms are often used interchangeably, but there are differences we will address in this chapter. Also, many investors assume that these strategies focus solely on environmental issues and do not appreciate the importance of the E, S, and G (environmental, social, and governance) pillars or these strategies' long-term historical returns.

This chapter discusses the growth of sustainable investing and the factors driving that growth. It shares research on short- and long-term results, discusses the importance of the ESG pillars, and provides a breakdown of assets under management.

LEADING THE CHANGE

A few organizations have provided leadership in addressing the challenges the world faces, from climate change to social inequality and resource scarcity. The United Nations published its Sustainability Development Goals (SDG) as a blueprint for a sustainable future. In it, the organization addresses the 17 global challenges we all face:

1. Poverty
2. Hunger
3. Health and well-being
4. Education
5. Gender equality
6. Clean water and sanitation
7. Affordable and clean energy
8. Decent work and economic growth
9. Industry, innovation, and infrastructure
10. Reduced inequalities
11. Sustainable cities and communities
12. Responsible consumption and production
13. Climate action
14. Life below water
15. Life on land
16. Peace, justice, and strong institutions
17. Partnerships for goals

Adopted in 2015 by 193 countries, the Sustainability Development Goals emerged from comprehensive negotiations across multiple nations, to inspire people from across sectors, geographies, and cultures. The UN Foundation's goal is to end extreme poverty, reduce inequality, and protect the planet by 2030. The SDG's imperative is to "leave no one behind" and is backed by evidence, practical commitments, and action.

The Forum for Sustainable and Responsible Investment (US SIF) is one of the leading voices for the advancement of sustainable and impact investing across all asset classes. Its mission is to educate investors and rapidly shift investment practices toward sustainability, focusing on long-term investment and the generation of positive social and environmental impacts. The US SIF publishes a biennial report highlighting sustainability trends.

Over the past couple of years, there has been a seismic shift in the way that companies address sustainability, beginning with a bold statement by the Business Roundtable in August 2019. It announced a new statement, signed by 181 CEOs who committed to lead their companies for the benefit of all stakeholders: customers, employees, suppliers, communities, and shareholders. This statement sent a message to corporate America that a company's focus must extend beyond merely generating profits and must include all stakeholders.

In a 2020 letter to clients, Larry Fink, CEO of Blackrock, the world's largest asset manager, introduced several initiatives designed to address sustainable investing.[1]

> BlackRock announced a number of initiatives to place sustainability at the center of our investment approach, including making sustainability integral to portfolio construction and risk management; exiting investments that present a high sustainability-related risk, such as thermal coal producers; launching new investment products that screen fossil fuels; and strengthening our commitment to sustainability and transparency in our investment stewardship activities.

In another bold move, in December 2020, Nasdaq announced that it wants to require the more than 3,000 companies listed on its exchange to have female and minority representation on their boards,[2] challenging the white-male-dominated composition of most corporate leadership.

Board diversity is more than just popular rhetoric. It leads to different perspectives and is good for a company. Studies have shown that board diversity leads to stronger financial results, more diverse views, and better checks and balances. Companies also need to promote women and minorities into other leadership positions at higher rates, with more mentoring and training geared to creating diverse organizations, with diverse points of view.

This movement has been fueled by concerns regarding climate change, social unrest related to the killing of George Floyd, and the "MeToo" movement, to name just a few catalysts. Institutions and individuals are raising their voices, and aligning their purposes and portfolios, to affect corporate change. This transformation has been decades in the making, but now there is a sense of urgency in addressing these issues.

DEFINING THE MARKETPLACE

In the 1990s, SRI became a convenient way to express views about unpopular activities. Investors opposing apartheid could exclude companies doing business in South Africa from their portfolios. Investors could express their displeasure with tobacco, alcohol, or gaming by excluding sin stocks or eliminating companies that damaged the environment from their client portfolios. Excluding these companies often meant sacrificing returns, however, so many investors shied away from socially responsible investing.

In the past couple of years, ESG screening has become increasingly popular with large institutions, HNW families, women, and millennials. This relative screening methodology assigns the highest weights to companies that exhibit the best practices. Multiple studies have shown that these strategies have historically outperformed their comparable unconstrained indices.

Sustainable investing—a broad descriptor that includes socially responsible investing, environmental, social, and governance, and impact investing—has grown substantially. According to the US SIF biennial report,[3] the total US assets under management for sustainable investing grew from $12 trillion in 2018 to $17.1 trillion in 2020, an increase of 42 percent. This represents nearly one-third of the US professional assets under management, an astounding 25-fold increase, or 14 percent annualized growth rate, since 1995. That's a significant accomplishment, especially given the skepticism of just a few years ago.

The report breaks down the sustainable investing assets under management at the beginning of 2020 into mutual funds (>$3 trillion), other commingled funds ($865 billion), alternative investments ($716 billion), ETFs ($21 billion), variable annuity ($17 billion), and other investment vehicles ($11.5 trillion). The last group includes UCITs and separately managed accounts.

The number of alternative investment sustainable investing vehicles grew. The US SIF 2020 trends report identified $716 billion in ESG assets under management across 905 alternative investment vehicles at the start of 2020, representing a 22 percent increase in assets compared to 2018, and a 16 percent increase in the number of funds. Private equity and venture capital ESG funds represent the largest number of alternative funds and increased 21 percent to 681 funds. Assets under management increased 55 percent to $438 billion.

If we dig into client segments, we see that sustainable investing by family offices increased 50 percent, from $4 billion to $6 billion, over the past two years. In 2020, the top issues for family offices were climate change, carbon emissions, and clean technology. Educational institutions held $378 billion in sustainably invested assets at the start of 2020—an increase of 19 percent from 2018—with a focus on climate change and carbon emissions.

The largest segment of sustainably invested money is in public funds: roughly $3.4 trillion, or a 10 percent increase over 2018.

Public funds include assets managed for federal, state, county, and municipal governments, including public employee pension plans such as CalPERS and CalSTRS. The report identified 181 public funds subject to various sustainability criteria, roughly the same as in 2018. The criteria focused on restricting investments in companies doing business with conflict-risk countries like Sudan and Iran. They also consider labor issues, board issues, tobacco, and climate change.

Proxy Voting

Asset managers can effect change by investing in companies with sound practices, diverse boards, and strong environmental practices; they can also vote proxies to ensure alignment around values and purpose. With the growth of sustainable investing, proxy voting has taken on greater importance for effecting governance changes, board diversity, and overall sustainability issues. Sustainable-investing-specific shareholder resolutions center on topics such as climate change, cybersecurity, data protection, online surveillance, content governance, diversity, environmental stewardship, sustainable governance, gender pay equity, human rights, lobbying, political spending, reputational product risks (opioids and guns), and workplace sexual harassment.

Morningstar has tracked the proxy voting records of large asset managers to see if they are effecting positive change and supporting positive resolutions. According to its recent report on climate change,[4] four of the five top asset managers failed to support 50 percent of the climate resolutions in 2020. Four of the five largest asset managers have sustainable investing strategies; yet the two largest asset managers, Blackrock and Vanguard, only supported 12 percent and 15 percent (respectively) of climate change resolutions.

Proxy voting provides another avenue to bring about change, but apparently many large asset managers are not voting in line with their mandates. This is because they have both sustainable and nonsustainable funds. In Larry Fink's January 2020 letter to shareholders, he stated, "We are facing the ultimate long-term problem. . . . Every government, company, and shareholder must confront climate change." However, Blackrock, the world's largest asset manager, missed the opportunity to effect change.

I suspect there will be a lot more attention to proxy voting in the future. This provides an opportunity to make positive changes, from climate change to board diversity and political spending. Large asset managers have a fiduciary obligation to vote proxies, but many are either neglecting their obligation or failing to vote in accordance with their stated discipline.

THE ROLE OF THE WEALTH ADVISOR

A 2019 study by New York Life Investments found that "only 20% of investors surveyed had financial advisors who recommended using an ESG strategy, while 38% of the respondents said they had an 'extremely high interest' in discussing these strategies with their financial advisor."[5] Wealth advisors need to become better versed in the nuances of various sustainable strategies and available investing options. Substantive differences exist between socially responsible investing (negative screening), ESG (relative screening), and impact investing (effecting change), though they all fall under the sustainable-investing umbrella. Advisors should help investors navigate the various strategies and identify the most appropriate solutions as part of an evolved consulting process. Figure 8.1 describes the various approaches, characteristics, and types of investments.

Wealth advisors should take the lead in educating investors about the merits of sustainable investing and how these strategies can be incorporated in portfolios. Wealth management is not about maximizing returns, but rather about making sure that a strategy provides the highest probability of achieving a client's goals. Those goals may include aligning the investor's purpose and portfolio. With millennials and Gen Z investors representing a larger percentage of the workforce, and as these generations begin to accumulate more wealth, advisors need to engage investors around sustainable

FIGURE 8.1 Sustainable Investing Spectrum

	Minimize Negative Impact		Target Impact	
	Restriction Screening	**ESG Integration**	**Thematic Exposure**	**Impact Investing**
Impact Priorities	Managing exposures by intentionally avoiding investments generating revenues from objectionable activities, sectors, or geographies	Proactively considering ESG criteria alongside financial analysis to identify opportunities and risks during investment process	Focusing on themes and sectors dedicated to solving sustainability-related domestic and global challenges	Allocating to investment funds focused on private enterprises structured to deliver positive social and/or environmental impacts
Characteristics	Differentiated by restriction criteria and degree of shareholder advocacy Not proactively seeking environmental and social impact	Differentiated by ESG integration process and degree of shareholder advocacy May also include screens	Differentiated by macroanalysis, sustainability, research, and sector focus	Differentiated by impact approach, regional focus, liquidity, and impact reporting May have investor restrictions
Investment Examples	Mutual fund that excludes companies from buy universe (e.g., tobacco, firearms, coal-mining companies)	Separately managed account incorporating analysis of ESG performance into stock selection process	Exchange-traded fund tracking index of renewable energy companies	A private equity fund focused on emerging consumers or project level renewable energy investment
		Public and Private Markets		**Private Markets**

investing. If wealth advisors fail to address these issues, millennials and Gen Z investors may feel compelled to find advisors who have similar values and perspectives.

According to a McKinsey report,[6] an unprecedented amount of assets will shift into the hands of US women over the next three to five years, creating a $30 trillion opportunity by the end of the decade. Today, women control roughly a third of the overall wealth, or $11 trillion in assets, and will likely inherit additional wealth as their older spouses pass. Women tend to make different investment decisions than their male counterparts. They are often more risk-averse and are more focused on achieving life goals. Multiple studies have shown that women consider social, environmental, and political issues in making decisions.

HNW investors are often focused on their legacy and giving back to society. Incorporating some form of sustainable investing can further their causes. Wealth advisors need to inquire about a family's passions and determine whether these should be incorporated in the family's portfolio. Inquiring about these interests also demonstrates the scope of capabilities. An HNW family may not perceive sustainability as part of an advisor's expertise and value proposition.

COMPARING THE RESULTS

Sustainable investing can offer strong returns. According to first-quarter 2020 Morningstar data,[7] "The returns of 70% of sustainable equity funds ranked in the top halves of their categories and 44% ranked in their category's best quartile." In addition, 24 out of 26 sustainable index funds outperformed their conventional counterparts. These results should not be surprising. Good companies, with sound policies and engaged employees, should do better over time.

We can draw some intuitive conclusions from the short-term results. During the global pandemic, oil prices plummeted, and people did not travel, eat in restaurants, or go on vacation—but there is much more to this story. Sustainable investment screening is designed to identify companies with strict environmental policies, engaged employees, and strong corporate governance (checks and balances). It helps identify good companies.

Because sustainable strategies have been adopted in Europe for many years, it is instructive to consider research conducted by Morningstar,[8] evaluating the results of 745 European-based sustainable funds, over 1, 3, 5, and 10 years. The research found that nearly 60 percent outperformed their unconstrained equivalent over the past 10 years, debunking the myth that sustainable funds underperform. Also, 77 percent of funds available 10 years ago still exist today, while only 46 percent of traditional funds available 10 years ago are still around.

MSCI research has shown that ESG screening affects valuations, risks, and the performance of underlying indices.[9] Strong ESG companies typically exhibit above-average risk controls and compliance standards. Better risk control standards mean that companies are less likely to experience fraud, embezzlement, and litigation. Less-frequent and severe risks also lead to fewer stock-specific tail risks. (See Figure 8.2.)

FIGURE 8.2 **Strong ESG Profile: Valuations, Risks, and Performance**

MSCI research also showed that companies with a strong ESG profile are more competitive than their peers, with more efficient use of capital, better human capital development, and better innovation. Strong, ESG companies use their competitive advantage to generate better returns. That leads to higher profitability, and higher profitability means better dividends. (See Figure 8.3.)

FIGURE 8.3 **Strong ESG Profile: Competitive Advantage**

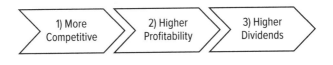

1) More Competitive → 2) Higher Profitability → 3) Higher Dividends

Companies with a strong ESG profile are less vulnerable to systematic market shocks and therefore show lower systematic risk. For example, these companies are often less vulnerable to spikes in commodity prices. Lower systematic risk generally means that a company has lower beta and therefore investors require a lower rate of return. This translates into a lower cost of capital, which leads to a higher valuation. (See Figure 8.4.)

FIGURE 8.4 **Higher Valuations**

1) Low Systematic Risk → 2) Low Cost of Capital → 3) High Valuation

SELECTING THE RIGHT STRATEGY

Because of advisor and investor interest, a plethora of new sustainable investing products—mutual funds, ETFs, and SMAs—have come to the market over the past several years. Investors need guidance in selecting the right solutions. Key considerations include:

- Do you gain exposure via an active or passive strategy?
- What experience does the portfolio management team have?

- How long have they been managing sustainable portfolios?
- How do they screen and weight securities?
- What is the historical track record?

When considering sustainable investing, wealth advisors often focus much of their attention on the environment and do not always consider the merits of the social and governance pillars of ESG. Individually, each helps in identifying good companies with sound policies and practices. Collectively, asset managers and index providers combine the E, S, and G in a portfolio. The weighting across pillars may depend on each industry or may be optimized to provide a particular outcome.

Environmental screening identifies companies focused on issues such as climate change, energy consumption, the use of natural resources, and reduction of their carbon footprints, among other issues. These companies typically have policies for dealing with the environment, consuming energy, and disposing of waste.

Social screening identifies companies with strong employee engagement, good human rights track records, broad employee diversity, and fair labor practices. These companies recognize the value of diversity and the need to embrace employee differences. They proactively promote minorities, often encourage mentoring, and engage their communities.

Governance screening identifies companies with independent and diverse boards, fair compensation practices, and strong checks and balances. They encourage independent points of view and strong boards of directors. Their disciplined risk management typically lets them avoid reputational risks.

These are independent pillars. A company may have a high E score and a low S score, or a high G score and a low E score. A firm might have a diverse board and strong social policies, but produce fossil fuels; it could hire and promote minorities but lack diversity on its board. A company that scores well across the E, S, and G pillars likely exhibits strong social policies and procedures, a track record of caring for the environment, and good corporate governance.

It is also important to consider how these pillars are weighted and incorporated. Much like traditional indexing, there can be dramatic differences between equally weighting the pillars, market-cap weighting, or using some form of optimization. The combination of pillars produces a diversified portfolio of companies.

MSCI deconstructed the performance of ESG ratings[10] and found that the top-quintile ESG companies outperformed the overall market from December 2006 to December 2019. MSCI research showed that the E, S, and G all outperformed the market, and the equally weighted ESG dramatically outperformed the individual pillars. MSCI also analyzed the return versus risk results by regions: World, North America, Europe, and Pacific. The ESG results exceeded the individual pillars across all regions. In other words, the sum of the parts exceeded the individual constituents.

Beware of Greenwashing

With the incredible growth of sustainable investing options, many asset managers are evaluating launching new strategies and/or repositioning existing strategies. Greenwashing (also called "green sheen"), where companies are primarily interested in raising money rather than in having an environmental impact, is becoming more of a concern.

> Greenwashing is the process of conveying a false impression or providing misleading information about how a company's products are more environmentally sound. Greenwashing is considered an unsubstantiated claim to deceive consumers into believing that a company's products are environmentally friendly.
>
> —Investopedia

There are several different types of greenwashing, including:

- **Environmental imagery.** Using images of leaves and animals, plus green packaging, can indicate greenwashing.
- **Misleading labels.** Certain products are labeled "Certified" or "100% organic" without any proof or supportive information.
- **Hidden trade-offs.** Companies put on an act of being environmentally friendly and sustainable, but the business may have hidden, unfriendly aspects. For example, a company may use "natural" or "recycled" materials, but the goods are manufactured using child labor.
- **Irrelevant claims.** A label might say that the product is free of certain chemicals, when in fact those chemicals are banned by law.
- **Lesser of two evils.** With this common practice, a company's claim may be true but doesn't erase the product's greater health or environmental risk. Organic cigarettes are one example.

For asset managers, greenwashing can involve claiming to incorporate sustainable screening but not following acceptable guidelines, or making misleading claims about the investment team's tenure and experience. There are firms with well-established teams and disciplines dedicated to sustainable investing, and those that are greenwashing to gain market share.

According to *Pensions & Investments*, investors have $40.5 trillion globally in sustainable assets, a number that's nearly doubled in four years.[11] These strategies are now available to institutions, large families, and retail investors, offered in separately managed accounts, mutual funds, and ETFs. *Pensions & Investments'* research showed that roughly 75 percent of the assets are actively managed. Still, more passive options are a growing trend, accounting for 60 percent of new asset flows in 2019.

As previously noted, not all strategies are created equal. There are differences in screening and weighting methodologies, the universes of underlying securities, definitions, and data sources. These differences can lead to dramatically divergent results over time.

As with consumer products, sustainable investment products should be truthfully labeled. Firms should be transparent about how they evaluate sustainability and how they use sustainable investments to build portfolios. With an influx of new strategies coming to the marketplace, investors should question newer strategies to determine whether their process truly incorporates sustainability screening. Review the company culture and practices, the investment team's tenure and track, as well as the underlying portfolio holdings.

Review public companies' underlying ESG score. Does the company incorporate sound E, S, and G practices? Is it focused on reducing its carbon footprint? Does it have diverse leadership and boards? What are the company demographics? Does it have sufficient checks and balances?

Advisors can serve a critical role in educating investors and vetting strategies. They can help tell the difference between firms and strategies that have committed to sustainable investing, and those that are using some form of greenwashing to capture assets.

THE STATE OF CHANGE

On President Joseph Biden's first day in office, he established how his administration will tackle climate change. He assembled a deep and dedicated team focused on global warming and installed policy experts at the State Department, the National Security Council, the Treasury Department, the Transportation Department, and the Office of the Vice President. Within hours of being sworn in as the 46th president, he signed executive orders rejoining the Paris Climate Agreement and canceling the Keystone Pipeline permit.

Even before taking office, Biden announced that he would name former Secretary of State John Kerry to the role of climate czar, a new position on the National Security Council. He also is expected to begin the process of forcing agencies to calculate the cost of carbon dioxide emissions to society. By pointing out the costs of climate change, the Biden administration hopes to change the cost-benefit analyses in a way that makes strong regulatory action more economically appealing and less susceptible to negative court rulings. Although he has avoided using the term "Green New Deal" for political reasons, President Biden has made it clear that he views climate change as one of the existential challenges facing our planet.

We should expect more climate-friendly policies and a growing awareness regarding each company's sustainability footprint. Wealth advisors can no longer ignore sustainable investing; they need to become proficient in explaining *what* it is and *how* it works. They will be expected to describe the pros and cons of the various approaches and have an informed point of view of how to incorporate sustainable investing in client portfolios.

PUTTING SUSTAINABILITY INTO PRACTICE

In the next several years, much more attention will focus on each company's carbon footprint, social practices, governance, and oversight. Companies the market sees as environmentally friendly may trade at substantial premiums. Just look at the valuation of Tesla and other companies in the electric vehicle (EV) ecosystem. Tesla's market capitalization is now larger than that of GM, Ford, Toyota, Volkswagen, Nissan, Honda, Hyundai, Fiat Chrysler, and Peugeot, even though Tesla accounts for less than 1 percent of total auto sales.

Companies in sectors the market sees as environmentally unfriendly, such as traditional automobile manufacturers and energy (oil and coal), will trade at depressed valuations, while alternative and renewable energy will receive premium pricing. Similarly, companies with sound diversity and labor practices will be able to recruit and retain talented people, while those with a poor history of hiring and promoting diverse candidates will struggle to attract talent.

Wealth advisors need to become more aware of each company's sustainability footprint. Whether they build portfolios for clients or work with third-party managers, they will need to understand how to screen and evaluate companies and managers. As with alternative investments, I recommend incorporating sustainable investing into the consulting process, rather than treating it as a separate decision. Wealth advisors should inquire about a family's interest in sustainability during the discovery process and should address it in the initial planning session if a client has expressed an interest. Advisors should screen managers for a track record in managing sustainable assets and ensure that they have a dedicated team, a sound investment process, and a history of delivering strong risk-adjusted results.

It may be challenging to find managers with long track records, or there may be better investment options that do not require sustainability screening. Not every manager and asset class needs to adhere to sustainability guidelines to do good. The initial planning session may provide parameters for the percentage of assets that must be sustainably focused and/or the types of assets that may be exempt from these guidelines.

In quarterly client reviews, advisors should both review performance results and report on the portfolio's alignment with the family's purpose. Rather than dwelling on short-term performance, wealth advisors should use the opportunity to focus on both the alignment between portfolio and purpose and on progress relative to the family's goals.

As you select an asset manager or fund, know that substantive differences exist between the screening methodologies that MSCI, FTSE Russell, Refinitiv, and Sustainalytics use. Asset managers may also develop their own methodology for screening and weighting securities. You may be surprised to learn that some funds own objectionable companies with higher sustainability scores than their peers: Chevron, Wells Fargo, and GM, for instance.

Incorporate a checklist that addresses these questions:

- What is the underlying universe of eligible securities?
- What is the screening and weighting methodology used?
- What is the weighting across pillars?
- What has been the historical performance (return and risk)?
- What is the portfolio management team's experience (for active managers)?

Sustainable investing presents an opportunity for advisors to demonstrate their value as educators and knowledgeable sources of information. Investors want help in understanding these strategies and better aligning their values and portfolios. As previously mentioned, women, millennials, Gen Z, and many HNW families care deeply about sustainable investing, and they need help navigating the confusing terminology and vast differences between one strategy and the next.

Wealth advisors need to become better versed in these strategies. They need to learn how to evaluate available options and help their clients align their portfolios with their purpose and values. In short, advisors need to help their clients navigate the various types of strategies and identify the most appropriate solution(s).

HNW investors who are interested in learning more about sustainable investing, or who want to align purpose and portfolio, may want to select a wealth advisor who understands and incorporates sustainable investing. Investors may want to inquire about the wealth advisory teams' experience in screening and investing in sustainable funds, and how many of their clients use some form of sustainable investing. If this is important to you, you should select an advisory team that values it as well.

CHAPTER 9

Goals-Based Investing

*At some elementary level, it is not hard to understand
intuitively that there is more to a family than its bank and
brokerage account.*

Jean Brunel
*Goals-Based Wealth Management:
An Integrated and Practical Approach to Changing
the Structure of Wealth Advisory Practices*

THROUGHOUT THIS BOOK, I HAVE DISCUSSED THE MERITS OF GOALS-based investing as a more evolved asset allocation approach. Goals-based investing addresses some of the limitations of modern portfolio theory (MPT) and blends attributes of behavioral finance, to solve for investors' needs, wants, and desires. In this chapter, I reframe the merits of goals-based investing, discuss how wealth advisors can incorporate it into their process, and provide a case study to bring the concept to life.

MPT has helped advisors and investors understand the advantages of diversification by minimizing risk, with the correlation across asset classes serving as the "secret sauce." However, MPT is built on several flawed assumptions, including the notion that investors are rational and will select the optimal portfolio. MPT relies upon historical return, risk, and correlation data to design the optimal combination of asset classes to either maximize returns for a given level of risk or minimize the risk for a desired level of return.

But what if equity returns and bond yields are lower in the future? What if the correlations across asset classes remains elevated? Unfortunately, using flawed or outdated data may mean that investors fall short of both their return and income requirements. This is precisely the environment we find ourselves in, with capital market assumptions projecting substantially lower returns and income over the next 10 to 20 years. Correlation data has been steadily rising due to the interconnectivity of the global markets.

MPT is mathematically driven, with the inputs determining the outputs. Behavioral finance is emotional, focusing on how investors respond to stimuli. Goals-based investing recognizes that investors are often solving for multiple goals simultaneously, and maximizing returns may not be one of those goals. Goals-based investing moves the wealth advisor's discussion from outperforming the market to achieving client goals. Goals-based investing aligns the portfolio allocation to specific goals. Mean-variance optimization is designed to maximize returns for a given level of risk or minimize the risk for a given return target and has certain built-in limitations.

Goals-based investing is designed to increase the likelihood of achieving life goals: accumulating wealth, generating income in retirement, saving for college, giving to charities, or some other specific outcome. HNW families pass on wealth from generation to generation through trusts, and they often fund numerous charitable activities. They may have multiple account types with different goals and objectives for each. Goals-based investing provides the flexibility of solving for multiple goals across multiple portfolios.

GOALS-BASED WEALTH MANAGEMENT

Goals-based wealth management marries financial planning and investment planning, providing a road map for investors in achieving their goals. Goals-based wealth management begins with the discovery process, trying to understand the HNW family's objectives. Where the traditional approach is to solve for multiple family needs in one portfolio, goals-based investing provides a framework for solving multiple goals, with different cash-flow needs and time horizons, with multiple portfolios. (See Figure 9.1.)

FIGURE 9.1 Global Wealth Management Process

Discovery process. What are the family's needs and wants? What are the various account types? What is unique about each account type?

Reviewing trust and estate issues. What types of trusts have been established (living, revocable, irrevocable, generation skipping, etc.)? How are assets distributed? Who receives them (children, grandchildren, charity, etc.)?

Establishing goals and objectives. What are you solving for (per account type)? What are the cash-flow needs and various time horizons?

Developing asset allocations. What are the return objectives for each account type, the income requirements, the time horizon to achieve the various goals, and the liquidity requirements?

Selecting the right investments. Which fund or manager can generate the required outcome? What are the structural trade-offs among mutual fund, ETF, separately managed account, registered fund, or private fund? How should you incorporate active and passive strategies? What role do alternative investments play in this diversified portfolio?

Monitoring progress relative to goals. How are the managers and accounts doing relative to their stated goals? Have there been changes to the family's circumstances? Do you need to make portfolio adjustments?

Advisors who adopt a goals-based wealth management process must be consistent in measuring progress relative to goals. They cannot fall into the trap of emphasizing performance in rising markets and goals-based investing in challenging environments. Their performance measurement tools need to evolve to report progress appropriately, rather than emphasizing performance relative to the S&P 500 or some other arbitrary benchmark.

The Means to the Ends

A client's portfolio is the *means to an end*. It's how their wealth grows over time and how they achieve their desired outcomes. Adopting a goals-based approach does not mean that wealth advisors should ignore performance, but rather change the utility function to solve for a family's objectives. HNW families obviously want and expect access to the best investment strategies. However, if the top-performing strategies come with high volatility and high turnover, then their value may be negated on an after-tax basis.

If assembled correctly, portfolios can solve for specific goals, and if you properly understand the role of each investment, you can measure its effectiveness in the overall portfolio. As covered throughout the book, I tend to think of asset classes as puzzle pieces. If they fit together well, they provide a clear picture of what the portfolio is designed to do. If they are put together in a haphazard fashion, the portfolio's purpose will not be clear. (See Figure 9.2.)

FIGURE 9.2 A Goals-Based Framework

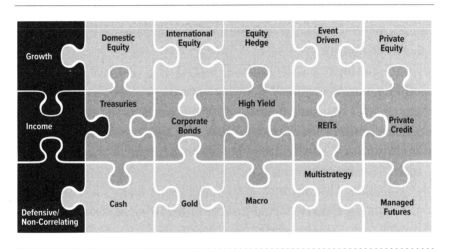

This puzzle piece analogy works well with clients because it helps demystify the individual investments and establish their role in a diversified portfolio. It is more intuitive for clients if we frame the investments in terms that they understand, such as growth, income, and defense. This framework establishes a more effective way of measuring each investment's success and failure. Gold (for instance) is not in the portfolio to outperform the S&P 500. It is a defensive asset, included in a portfolio to provide safety and stability in the face of market shocks. Fixed income, as the name suggests, is designed to generate income in portfolios, and equity-oriented strategies provide capital appreciation.

Growth. In a traditional sense, portfolio growth comes from its equity allocation: large, small, international, and emerging markets. The list can also include private equity, equity-hedge, and event-driven strategies.

Income. We typically think of diversified bonds—treasuries, corporate, government, and high-yield bonds—as a portfolio's primary source of income. Investors with the necessary liquidity may want to consider private credit, nontraded REITs, or distressed strategies.

Defensive. We typically consider cash, gold, and treasuries as defensive assets during periods of elevated volatility and market corrections. HNW investors may also want to consider macro, multistrategy, and real assets to buffer volatility and provide downside protection.

By framing the asset class discussion like this, advisors can move investors from benchmarking everything to the S&P 500 in rising markets and to cash in falling markets. Wealthy families may own many of the same asset classes across account types, but may weight the accounts differently to achieve the various goals. A trust established for grandchildren may be more growth-oriented because of their long time horizon. The patriarch's retirement account may be geared toward generating income, and the personal account may be more defensive, based on their views of the prevailing market environment.

If we focus on specific goals by asset class, then we should use the correct metrics to evaluate the effectiveness of the various asset classes. For the portfolio's growth-oriented component, we focus on the return-risk trade-off. For the income-oriented component, we measure each asset class's yield. For defensive assets, we examine the correlation of each asset class relative to the S&P 500, because we are trying to reduce the overall portfolio's equity beta.

These are not the only metrics to consider. For the income component, we must recognize that different risks are associated with treasuries, high yield, and private credit, and also acknowledge different risks associated with public and private equities. Big differences can exist from one strategy to the next, especially as we consider alternative investments.

Defining Risk

In his 2005 paper, Ash Chhabra defined the three dimensions of risk as "personal," "market," and "aspirational."[1] Personal risk is the possibility that we might fail to achieve a given standard of living; to ameliorate this risk, we focus on reducing downside risk, potentially accepting below-market returns to reduce risk. We generally focus on market risk, balancing risk and reward through a diversified portfolio to sustain a lifestyle. Aspirational risk means that investors would be willing to take on somewhat more risk to enhance their lifestyles.

The personal bucket should focus on protecting assets and will accept below-market returns. The market bucket's risks and returns should track the market. The aspirational bucket should target expected returns above the market and be willing to take on slightly more risk to achieve those results.

Unfortunately, traditional finance focuses on volatility or standard deviation as the preferred risk measure. It does not distinguish between positive and negative volatility. From our behavioral finance discussion, we know that investors feel very differently about losses and gains, and Kahneman and Tversky suggested that investors would go to great lengths to avoid losses. If investors are opposed to experiencing losses, wealth advisors should build that into investor goals and should target downside protection in selecting investment options.

FAMILY GOALS

HNW and UHNW families are typically solving for multiple goals simultaneously and are not focused solely on maximizing returns. Their goals may include preserving wealth, transferring wealth efficiently, and funding causes that matter to the family. A family's wealth may determine priorities, and it may be instructive to review the hierarchy of financial needs (Figure 9.3).

FIGURE 9.3 **Hierarchy of Financial Needs**

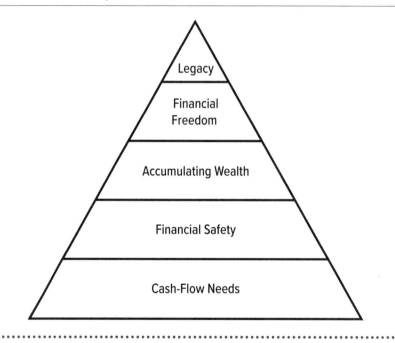

Cash-flow needs. Meeting the basic needs for food and shelter.

Financial safety. The ability to create a financial cushion for unforeseen events.

Accumulating wealth. Building wealth, saving for retirement, and paying down debt.

Financial freedom. Adequate savings for retirement, children's educations, and vacations.

Legacy. Focused on estate planning, tax planning, charitable giving, and instilling value in children and grandchildren.

Consider a hypothetical HNW family (see Figure 9.4). Tom and Patricia have two children, Charlie and Samantha. Charlie has three children and is focused on saving for their college expenses and traveling with the family. Samantha has a young daughter with special needs. Tom and Patricia have set up trusts for the children and grandchildren to help them achieve their respective goals.

FIGURE 9.4 Hypothetical HNW Family

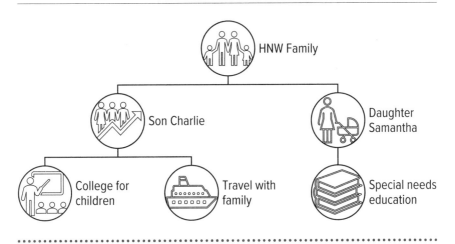

An advisor might treat this HNW family as a single relationship, but their respective goals and objectives will likely be different depending upon the respective dollar amounts, cash-flow needs, and time horizons. Each account should have its own goals and a customized portfolio designed to meet those goals.

Sustainable Investing

Increasingly, HNW investors are seeking to align their purposes and portfolios, including some form of sustainable investing for some or all their portfolios. Wealth advisors need to recognize this growing trend and inquire about the family's interests in supporting causes such as the environment, social issues, gender equality, healthcare, and board diversity. Advisors should determine whether these preferences should be incorporated into the family's portfolios.

As previously discussed, advisors should take the lead in educating investors about the merits of sustainable investing, explaining the confusing terminology and different screening methodologies. Sustainable investing is not a fad that is going away anytime soon. It is a way to identify good companies with sound practices. HNW families are focused on their legacies and want to instill values in their children. Aligning their portfolios and purposes is one way of expressing their values.

Wealth advisors will need to do more than just educate families about sustainable investing. They will need to identify a stable of managers who can help build sustainable portfolios. Depending on the size and specialization of a wealth advisory practice, it may make sense to designate someone as the sustainability specialist. The sustainability specialist could take the lead in educating families about sustainable investing and understanding the nuances of various managers. Because the landscape is changing so rapidly, the sustainability specialist could also stay abreast of industry trends, new products coming to the market, and how families are using these strategies effectively.

Even if the family does not incorporate sustainable investing, by inquiring about the family's interests the advisor gains unique insights into the family and changes the way the family views the wealth advisor's services and capabilities. At a minimum, every wealth advisory practice should have a baseline understanding of sustainable investing and a handful of managers that have been properly vetted.

ENGAGING HNW FAMILIES

Goals-based wealth management is designed to understand a family's various goals, often spanning multiple generations. To understand a family's ever-evolving needs, a wealth advisor must develop relationships with the entire family and the family's other trusted advisors. Too often, advisors develop strong ties to the patriarch and matriarch and fail to adequately engage the children. Eventually, the children will inherit from their parents. Without a strong relationship with their parents' advisor, they may seek a different advisor. Wealth advisors must develop relationships across the family. One way to develop trust is to help educate them about investing.

Scott Perry wanted in-person meetings with his trusted advisors and children so that we could educate his children and develop relationships with them. He wanted to help prepare his daughter for leading the family, so he wanted her to understand our investment philosophy and team. Scott was thinking about his family legacy and continuity from one generation to the next.

David Manning wanted to fully understand our investment philosophy and underlying investments, before allocating capital. He wanted to build a long-lasting relationship. He appreciated that I patiently helped him understand things that were relatively new to him. David later asked me to go through a similar process with his sister. I had earned his trust and so he referred me to someone he cared deeply about.

Educating families is often the best way to earn their trust. Jean Brunel suggested the need for a "financial interpreter"[2] to help educate families about investing principles and translate the field's jargon. I have always tried to lead with education and recognize that a family's balance sheet isn't a good gauge of members' investment acumen. There are several techniques to engage the entire family:

Engage children. Meet with adult children separately to develop personal relationships with them. Focus on understanding their interests and portfolio goals.

Educate family. Send family members reading material about finance or personal interests. Add personal notes: "Mary, I thought that you would find this book of interest given our recent discussion."

Develop personal relationships. Invite family to events outside the office: sporting events, concerts, dinners, wine tastings, and so on. Consider bringing your own family, to let the family see you in a different light.

Conduct family meetings. Offer to conduct family meetings or retreats. This is a great opportunity to be a trusted advisor while also observing family dynamics.

Develop a family mission statement. Many wealthy families have a *mission statement* that describes their purpose. It may be worthwhile to develop a mission statement for HNW families who do not already have one.

> A family mission statement is a combined, unified expression from all family members of what your family is all about— what it is you really want to do and be—and the principles you choose to govern your family life.
> —Stephen Covey, *The 7 Habits of Highly Effective Families*

Businesses often use mission statements to help sharpen their focus and align all employees around a common goal. A family mission statement serves a similar purpose, articulating the family's principles. The family mission statement expresses the family's values and can be used to evaluate decisions that impact the broader family. This is particularly important for multigenerational families where passing on these values from one generation to the next perpetuates the family's legacy.

A family mission statement is not about maximizing wealth, but rather about what the wealth lets the family do to further their passions and defining their purpose across generations.

INCORPORATING GOALS-BASED WEALTH MANAGEMENT

I began this book by suggesting that advisors should evolve their practices to better meet the growing needs of HNW investors, evolving from selling products to solving needs and expanding our capabilities to include trust and estate issues, dealing with concentrated positions, lending, and tax management. Goals-based wealth management provides the framework for addressing these needs.

Wealth advisors should adopt a goals-based wealth management approach to solve the needs of HNW families, changing their relationship and value proposition to better align with the family's goals. HNW families have complex needs, and goals-based wealth management is designed to identify them and then deal with them individually. Goals-based wealth management is the preferable model for both wealth advisors and HNW families.

Goals-based investing provides a road map for families large and small. Some families may be more focused on intergenerational wealth transfers, and others may be more focused on retirement planning. Some may be focused on charitable giving, while others are solving for college funding. Typically, HNW families are solving for multiple needs simultaneously, and their approach should be tailored to meeting each goal.

Wealth management is an ever-evolving set of disciplines. The one constant is serving the needs of families. Larger families often have more complexity and may require specialized team coverage. Wealth management is a multigenerational endeavor; therefore, it is incumbent on the advisor to develop relationships with the whole family to effectively deal with the inevitable wealth transfer challenges to come.

Family Offices

Family offices have considerable wealth and complexity to deal with, including investment management, charitable giving, tax management, and family dynamics, among others. Family offices typically leverage a network of trusted advisors to source opportunities and help address the challenges they face. However, they need to be careful that decisions are carefully considered across the family units. Family members often have different preferences and priorities, and they may act differently than their parents and siblings. Families can easily stray from their mission statement if it isn't constantly revisited and reinforced.

Family offices should periodically review their various objectives across the various family members and account types. It's easy for them to get out of sync with their stated goals when the market moves or circumstances change. Variation in underlying investments means that portfolios may be prone to big swings, with private equity, concentrated holdings, and other unique opportunities delivering oversized returns. Families may be hesitant to make portfolio adjustments due to tax consequences and may deviate from their original target allocations over time.

Family offices often go to great lengths to conceal their overall wealth and how their assets are allocated across multiple firms. This can lead to conflicting or overlapping strategies, and it requires careful coordination from the family office investment staff. I suggest that family offices adopt a goals-based wealth management approach. They can employ a combination of internal and external experts to help them address the family's needs, and they would do well to formalize the process.

HNW Investors

I have challenged wealth advisors to evolve their practices to address the needs of HNW investors. I also recognize that some HNW investors make their own investment decisions and do not engage advisors in the traditional sense. I think there are two primary types of HNW investors who don't hire advisors: those who come from the financial services industry and are knowledgeable about the markets, and those who do not value or trust financial advisors.

Many HNW investors have earned their wealth from the financial services industry: retired Wall Street investment bankers, real estate developers, Goldman Sachs partners, former CEOs, hedge fund managers, private equity investors—and that is just at my country club. These individuals are knowledgeable and well connected and are equipped to make many of their own investment decisions. They may need some help in areas outside their core competencies, but they likely do not need a wealth advisor as much as other investors. Even so, they benefit from formalizing their goals across family and account types (personal, retirement, trust, foundations, etc.).

Hopefully, these sophisticated HNW investors will embark on a *lifetime of learning,* as investment philosophy and products evolve. They will need to keep pace with an ever-changing market environment. I wrote this book with these investors in mind: friends who have been successful throughout their careers and possess great knowledge within their domains, but need to effectively integrate various solutions to achieve their goals.

I hope that these HNW investors will read my book and adopt a goals-based investing approach, leveraging advisors to find potential investment opportunities. I encourage investors of all sizes and sophistication to develop a process and stick to it in good times and bad. Remove the temptation to let emotions drive the decision-making process.

CASE STUDY: FAMILY OFFICE

I began my career working for a family office, and the lessons I learned have shaped my perspective throughout my career. My experiences working directly with the family can help illustrate how wealthy families think about solving for multiple goals across multiple accounts. Obviously, I have changed the family's name and some particulars.

The Adams family established a family office to serve their investment, tax, philanthropic, and estate-planning needs. The family built their wealth in the commodity business and had strong ties to many of the largest Wall Street firms. The family was focused on transferring wealth from one generation to the next and funding several causes, including hospitals and healthcare, cultural programs, social services, and youth programs.

We had a single floor in a new midtown Manhattan high rise that allowed for frequent interactions with the patriarch and his two sons. (His daughter periodically visited the office.) The office was featured in *Architectural Digest* because of the spectacular views, modern design, and impressive art collection. The staff was close, which was important for a team that constantly dealt with confidential information. We had holiday parties where the extended family would often attend. Over the years, I have remained close with several colleagues from those early days.

The family original made their wealth in the 1890s. Through smart investing, unique access, and a long-term focus the family had grown their wealth substantially over time. They would be considered "old money": multigenerational wealth. The opposite is "new money," often created by a company IPO. Old-money families are born into wealth and are typically more conservative. They focus on their legacy and maintain a low profile. New-money families tend to be more aggressive, are generally willing to take on more risk, and often flaunt their wealth.

The Adams family went to great lengths to protect the family and stay out of the spotlight, even as they gave generously to their favorite causes. The family shielded their identity by using the name of an old warehouse as the company name, unlike the Bloomberg, Bezos, or Gates family offices, which use their names freely. The Adamses hired a small cadre of trusted advisors to handle their investment, tax, and philanthropic needs.

I joined the family office as a young man from a small farm community with no formal investment training. This unique experience shaped my perspective on working with wealthy families. I learned many valuable lessons during my time working for the Adams family. Beyond developing an investment philosophy, I learned a great deal about tax planning, trust and estate issues, philanthropy, and working across generations.

I was never intimidated by a family's wealth, status, or accomplishments. I recognized that they had their own set of challenges, including trying to instill strong values in their children. I was always comfortable interfacing with billionaires, CEOs, entertainers, and professional athletes because I realized that their wealth did not define who they were. It was their experiences and values that distinguished them.

Jack Adams was the patriarch of the family. Jack's first wife had passed, and he later remarried Elizabeth. Jack had two sons, Patrick and Billy, and a daughter, Kelly, plus eight grandchildren between them. The family established a limited partnership, multiple trusts, and a charitable foundation. We had internal investment and tax expertise, and we leveraged outside experts as well, to deal with the family's far-reaching activities. Because the family's wealth traced back over a hundred years, we had a lot of low cost-basis stocks, and tax management was very important. Because of the family's wealth, and their relationships across Wall Street, we were constantly presented with unique investment opportunities, including hedge funds, private equity, and private real estate.

I share this background to show the diversity of this family's goals across various account types. The family limited partnership focused on sourcing unique investment opportunities. Because of the family's sophistication and long-term approach, they had the patience to let private equity and private real estate opportunities reach their potential. The children's personal accounts paid for multiple homes, grandchildren's education, and various charitable gifts. Consequently, their portfolios were geared toward capital appreciation. These needed to be more liquid than the limited partnership and the grandchildren's trust accounts, which had long time horizons. The charitable foundation funded the family's generous gifts and various causes. We wanted to grow the foundation to continue the good work and could make contributions to offset any shortfalls.

One of my most vivid memories of my time with the family office was on October 16, 1987—the Friday before Black Monday. I remember watching the market close down over 100 points for the first time, and I was fearful of what would happen when the market opened on Monday. I asked the president of the family office if he was considering selling anything. With his usual calm demeanor, he responded that the family's cost basis on many of its individual stocks were pennies on the dollar, and that panicking was never a winning strategy. The family thought about their wealth from one generation to the next and were truly long-term investors. I remember this lesson every time we experience a market correction.

The Adams family's story helps illustrate the diversity of goals that a family may be solving for and the need to customize the solutions based on those goals. The family had dozens of accounts, with different goals and time horizons, to achieve them. Taxes and gifting strategies were of critical importance, and asset location was as important as asset allocation. Because of the family's wealth, we were often approached about unique investment opportunities and could afford to tie up capital for an extended period of time if warranted. Not surprisingly, the family had healthy allocations to private equity, private real estate, and commodities and could leverage the biggest and best firm's on Wall Street to source opportunities.

Wealth advisors should break down a family's goals by account, rather than trying to solve for every goal with a single approach. In developing family goals, wealth advisors should consider each account's objectives, cash-flow needs, time horizon, tax status, gifting strategies, and risk profile. After establishing each account's goals, advisors should evaluate the most appropriate approach to achieving the goals, including asset allocation, asset location, tax management, and portfolio construction.

KEY TAKEAWAYS

In this chapter, we have explored some of the limitations of modern portfolio theory and explored how goals-based investing combines elements of MPT and behavioral finance. Goals-based investing is designed to identify and solve for multiple goals simultaneously. Rather than merely optimizing a portfolio to maximize returns or minimize risks, goals-based investing recognizes that HNW families have multiple goals, with different cash-flow needs, and different time horizons to achieve them.

A goals-based wealth management process provides the framework for capturing various goals across family accounts and developing the appropriate solutions for each account. Family goals are typically geared toward life events like transferring wealth, college funding, and charitable giving, each of which requires a dedicated focus to achieve the desired outcome. As discussed in this chapter, HNW families are increasingly considering sustainable investing, and wealth advisors need to understand and respond to this growing trend.

Wealth advisors need to engage all HNW family members and develop relationships with children, siblings, and other trusted advisors. I suggested a few tactics to engage wealthy families, including engaging the children, educating the family, conducting family meetings, developing personal relationships, and developing a family mission statement.

I emphasize the importance and relatability of the concepts covered in this chapter and throughout the book to family offices and HNW investors who choose to make their own decisions. Family offices and HNW investors should develop a goals-based wealth management process to identify and solve for family goals. UHNW and HNW families should leverage experts as they deem appropriate, tapping into such areas of expertise as financial planning, investment planning, tax management, and charitable giving. They can employ multiple experts or a consolidated provider to source unique investment opportunities like hedge funds, private equity, private credit, and real assets, among others.

UHNW and HNW investors want and expect access to the best ideas across multiple firms. The challenge is often tracking the progress relative to a family's multiple goals across the diverse set of providers. UHNW families with significant wealth (typically $250 million or more in investable assets) and complexities may choose to form a family office to manage and monitor their investment, tax, and philanthropic needs, while others may choose the scale of multifamily offices (MFOs) or other wealth advisory firms.

Lastly, I used a personal case study to illustrate the complexity of dealing with wealth across multiple generations and account types, and how the strategies need to be tailored to meet respective goals. I believe that there are valuable lessons in this case, whether you are dealing with UHNW families or smaller families with less complex needs.

Maximizing returns in isolation may not be prudent and may cause undue tax consequences, among other issues. Wealth advisors should take the time to develop a strategy based on the specific goals for each account, given their desired outcome, cash-flow needs, and time horizon. I have provided real client experiences throughout this book to help bring these concepts to life and emphasize the importance of developing personal relationships with families, moving beyond the portfolio.

CHAPTER 10

The Future of Wealth Management

By 2030, at least 80 percent of advisors will offer goal-based advice, and about half of clients will actively pursue and track bite-sized goals (such as saving for three college credits a month)— and this granular goal-tracking will span customers' investment, protection, education, retirement, and broader wellness.

McKinsey & Company
On the Cusp of Change:
North American Wealth Management in 2030

IT IS NOT A STRETCH TO IMAGINE THAT BY 2030, INVESTORS WILL use wearable technology to track progress relative to their goals, just as we monitor our health today with fitness trackers. This would not eliminate the role and value of advisors, but rather shift their focus to developing a comprehensive financial plan, establishing realistic objectives, implementing an investment strategy, and monitoring progress toward their goals. Technology is not a replacement for good advice, but a tool to provide efficiency and valuable information to help investors achieve their desired outcomes.

I began this book by discussing the ongoing transformation of the wealth management industry and how advisors must evolve their practices to meet their client's goals. I said that advisors needed to reframe their value proposition, integrating financial planning, investment planning, retirement planning, tax management, trust and estate issues, charitable giving, and potentially lending solutions.

Throughout this book, I discussed the limitations of MPT and suggested that goals-based investing represents a more evolved approach to allocating assets, marrying attributes of MPT and behavioral finance. I suggested that wealth advisors and HNW investors should consider a broader set of asset classes to meet a wider array of goals. Fortunately, product innovation has made it easier for many investors to access markets and asset classes that were once difficult.

The markets have transformed rapidly over the past 10 years, and we will likely see even more changes over the next decade. In this chapter, I explore the changes underway and make projections about other shifts that will reshape the wealth management industry:

- *What do the next 10 years hold for the wealth management industry?*
- *What are the implications for advisors and investors?*
- *What are some of the investment trends?*
- *How will advice be delivered and by whom?*
- *Which trends will shape the future of wealth management?*

THE FUTURE OF ADVICE

In the next 10 years, the industry will experience a transformation that will reshape how wealth management looks and responds to investor needs. I predict:

1. A demographic shift (younger and more diverse)
2. More dedicated teams
3. Technology as an enabler
4. Goals-based investing as the norm
5. ESG and direct indexing

6. Bifurcation of advice (robo and wealth advisor)
7. HNW investors demanding highly customized advice
8. The rise of the superteam
9. Advisors needing to *right-size* their practices
10. Introduction of advisor ratings

The advisors of the future will be younger and more diverse than ever before. They will embrace technology and align their portfolios and purpose. In the next 10 years, we will see a demographic shift across the wealth management industry, with women, minority, and millennial advisors growing at twice the rate of the overall industry. The growth will be driven by clients demanding to see more advisors who look like them and the aging demographics of practices dominated by white men. As wealth advisors continue to embrace a team structure to serve the needs of HNW investors, they will seek greater diversity across teams to better match their client base.

Younger advisors will recognize the importance of technology to provide scale and efficiency, and will not view it as a threat to their value proposition. Large wealth management firms will still invest heavily in technology as their margins continue to come under pressure. There will be a more pronounced bifurcation between highly customized and personalized advice for HNW investors and more digital advice offerings for smaller clients (financial planning, asset allocation, direct indexing).

Goals-based investing will become the norm, with technology evolving to more efficiently establish and track progress relative to multiple goals at the same time. Technology will also make it easier to align investor preferences in portfolios, whether that means incorporating sustainability screening or direct indexing: letting investors create their own basket of stocks. Women and millennials will continue to embrace sustainability and direct indexing, and the appeal will expand to other constituents as the benefits become more universally accepted.

Technological advancements and increased pressure on the advisor's economic model will push smaller investors toward robo-offerings.

These clients will likely only have access to a service center—no financial advisor. Large wealth management firms are already moving in this direction. Although technology provides efficiency, these firms cannot afford to pay advisors to provide a commoditized solution. Many studies have suggested that technology will mean a dramatic reduction in the number of advisors over the next couple of years, and many advisors will retire without adequate succession plans.

As tech-enabled solutions let wealth advisors serve more clients, more efficiently, HNW families will demand greater customization and integration to solve for their complex needs. Wealth advisors serving HNW investors will need dedicated teams with expertise across a range of disciplines: investment management, tax management, trust and estates, and handling concentrated positions. To provide the in-depth support necessary, wealth advisors will need to *right-size* their practices, determining how many HNW families they can handle well. There will be more superteams (six- or more person teams) at the wirehouses, and many will eventually go independent as they outgrow this model.

Advisor ratings on a range of issues—performance, service, investment expertise, and diversity of practice—will emerge. Investors will be able to scan the ratings to select the best advisor for them and will replace advisors by finding suitable alternatives in minutes. This can be both a threat and an opportunity, depending on how well an advisor is rated and how they adapt to this changing model.

Currently, several organizations rate wealth advisors and RIAs (Barron's, Wealthmanagement.com, FT, etc.), but firms typically pay to be included and nominate advisors, often based on practice size. Client satisfaction will likely drive future ratings, with reviews coming from clients and prospects via an app like Yelp, Expedia, or Groupon. The ratings will focus on what matters to clients: the team's expertise level, quality of services, resource depth, advisor empathy, and ability to achieve investor goals. Clients will determine ratings based on experience rather than firms paying to participate.

Trends and Opportunities

Several trends will play out over the next 10 years, including:

1. The RIA segment continues to grow.
2. Wealth management firms need to redefine their value proposition.
3. Wealth advisors gain power.
4. New economic models (subscription) develop.
5. New competitors emerge.

More and more advisors will consider going independent, either joining an RIA aggregator (Hightower, Focus Financial, or Mercer Advisors) or hanging out their own shingle to remove conflicts of interest and/or improve their economic model. These advisors will tout their independence, fiduciary status, and alignment in serving their clients. RIAs will also recognize that size provides efficiencies, and RIA consolidation will accelerate.

Wirehouses will not become obsolete in serving HNW investors but will need to reinvent themselves somewhat, emphasizing their advisor education initiatives, unique access to investments, and depth of resources. They will need to work harder to retain quality advisors, as the pendulum will shift in the advisor's favor in the coming years. Wealth advisors will have more options if they stay with their current firms or go independent. Investors will continue to question advisors' independence and economic value, and there will be greater scrutiny of fees.

The economic arrangements among wealth advisors, asset managers, and wealth management firms will come under pressure, and different pricing models will emerge to better align fees and value. According to a McKinsey report, "In 2030, up to 80 percent of new wealth management clients will want to access advice in a Netflix-style model—that is, data-driven, hyper-personalized, continuous, and, potentially, by subscription."[1]

I would not be surprised to see new competitors emerge, including firms from outside the financial services industry—Google,

Amazon, Apple, Walmart—especially for the lower end of the market. As the retail market is becoming more commoditized and tech-enabled, a nontraditional provider may be better equipped to emerge as a formidable competitor. The tech giants have shown a willingness to enter new markets and understand technology's value in meeting consumer demand. If retail investors do not value advisors and are consumed with finding the lowest price, it is not impossible to imagine that Amazon could develop a better algorithmic mousetrap, at a considerable discount to the market.

Investment Opportunities

From an investment perspective, we have seen some big changes over the past couple of years and likely will see a continuation of product innovation. Investment trends to watch over the next 10 years include the following:

1. The private market will become easier to access for a broader group of investors.
2. Hedge funds will reemerge but with reduced pricing.
3. Sustainable investing will become more mainstream.
4. Direct indexing and active ETFs will emerge as viable investment options.
5. Model portfolios will continue to evolve to meet advisor and investor demand.

As we have covered in this book, there are considerably more private companies than public companies, and I do not anticipate that trend reversing anytime soon. Private companies are remaining private longer because there are alternative sources of capital, and they are better able to execute their long-term strategy as a private company, rather than responding to shareholders' short-term demands.

With growing demand from HNW families and the product evolution to meet that demand, more private market opportunities will be available to a larger group of investors. Recognizing this demand, large asset managers and private equity firms have begun to offer these investments to a broader array of investors through feeder and registered funds. In a rare move, we have seen regulators acknowledge the need to make these valuable investments more readily available, including in retirement plans.

With the mainstreaming of private market investments, wealth advisors will need to take the lead in educating investors about the role these investments play in a diversified portfolio, as well as their structural trade-offs. The wealth advisor's value proposition will continue to shift from managing portfolios to serving as a quarterback and educator, bringing together the right pieces of the puzzle in appropriate weights.

In the next decade, hedge funds will come back into vogue as market volatility, greater disparity between the winners and losers, and rising geopolitical risks all reemerge. With their multifaceted approach to responding to market conditions, wealth advisors will need to understand the differences between strategies and combine them effectively to achieve their clients' goals. However, to gain broader acceptance from HNW investors, hedge fund strategies will need to have reduced fees and lower minimums.

Registered funds provide a bridge between the classic limited partnership structures and the more liquid structures available at lower minimums. But if they fail to provide returns that are comparable to their hedge fund and private market equivalents, investors will find other types of investments. Wealth advisors should expect to see some trade-offs in providing better liquidity, and managers will need to deliver high-quality products to the marketplace. By and large, the first generation of liquid alternatives were watered-down versions of hedge fund strategies and failed to deliver on their promise. Advisors and investors must be more discerning of structural trade-offs in the future.

As previously covered, sustainable investing has grown rapidly over the past couple of years, and it is becoming a much more mainstream investment approach. With more investments coming to the markets, and more technology being developed to analyze the underlying holdings, wealth advisors need to take the lead in educating investors and building out a stable of sustainable investment options. Investors are beginning to understand that screening and weighting securities based on sustainability helps identify good companies with sound policies regarding the environment, social issues, and board governance.

With the introduction of fractional shares and the growing interest in reflecting values in portfolios, direct indexing is poised for substantial growth in the next 10 years. Direct indexing lets investors customize their baskets of securities to reflect their views. Along with the rapid growth of active ETFs, these two vehicles can help stem the outflows that many active managers have experienced over the past decade or so. I am not sure that they are threats to the ever-evolving ETF marketplace, but rather as replacements for more expensive active management options. This is not to suggest the demise of active management. I am merely suggesting that the overall pie can grow by offering more investors more options. Good active managers will thrive, and other options will replace weaker ones.

The number of model providers, model diversity, and models' overall acceptance in the marketplace will continue to grow. Asset allocation models that can help investors achieve their goals will become increasingly valuable to wealth advisors and their clients, providing scale, efficiency, and better outcomes. As the model providers develop longer track records and more loyal adopters, this will become a much larger portion of asset managers' business. Open-architecture models should gain market share relative to proprietary-only models, as advisors demand the "best-of-the-best" solutions, and models will need to expand the number and type of underlying investments. Alternative investments would be a logical evolutionary step, but solving the differentiated fee issues may be challenging initially.

Two other investment trends could emerge in the next decade: Bitcoin and special purpose acquisition companies (SPACs). Bitcoin will continue to gain traction and will become accepted by hedge funds and individual investors, but I have a hard time seeing it as anything more than a speculative investment. It is not a commodity like gold or a currency like the dollar, and I think its price movement is driven more by supply and demand than by any fundamental valuation. Bitcoin and other cryptocurrencies will likely be used for payments and may eventually become regulated. Unfortunately, I am unable to develop an investment thesis that adequately describes how investors should use Bitcoin in their portfolios and how to properly value it. Therefore, I encourage wealth advisors and investors to proceed with caution.

Beginning in 2020 and growing through 2021, SPACs have flooded the financial markets. A SPAC is a company with no commercial operations that is formed strictly to raise capital through an IPO, for the purpose of acquiring an existing company. SPACs are also known as "blank check companies" because they begin without an operating business or stated acquisition target. SPACs have been around for decades, but they became increasingly popular in 2020, due in part to the euphoria associated with so many private companies with values of more than $1 billion going public. Of course, there are substantial differences between SPACs and traditional IPOs, primarily in the due diligence and disclosures.

Like direct listings, which represent another way to go public, SPACs will likely be around for a while. However, I am not convinced they will replace the typical IPO, and I worry that individual investors do not adequately understand the risks associated with this investment vehicle.

Wealth advisors can serve a critical role in educating investors about new and improved products and strategies coming to the market. Some will be beneficial and help in democratizing access to once-elusive investments; while others will fail to meet client expectations and will leave investors skittish about investing in the markets that seem to favor hedge funds, institutions, and family offices.

THE FUTURE OF WEALTH MANAGEMENT

The wealth management industry has evolved a great deal over the years. Every time someone has predicted its demise, the industry has reinvented itself and emerged with different ways of serving investors. When commissions were deregulated on May 1, 1975, the industry responded by introducing wrap-fee accounts and shifting toward advisory fees to better align with client interests. When the industry noticed that SMAs were inefficient and advisors found it difficult to get client permission for portfolio adjustments, the industry introduced discretionary programs that provided scale and efficiency in executing orders across multiple accounts, without requiring permission. When the industry noticed that advisors were struggling to integrate multiple wrap accounts, it invented the unified managed account (UMA) to capture family holdings more efficiently in a single account.

How will the industry respond to the new set of challenges? A few ways in which the industry may change over the next 10 years include these:

1. Wealth management division spin-offs
2. Education as the differentiator
3. Scale and efficiency at a premium
4. All firms offering commission-free trading
5. Artificial intelligence used to target services

Wealth Management Spin-off

With increased scrutiny regarding conflicts of interest, one or more wirehouses may spin off their wealth management divisions in the next 10 years. To improve overall economics, wealth management firms encourage advisors to cross-sell affiliated asset manager and banking products. Affiliated asset managers have had a tough time selling products to affiliated broker-dealers and will face increased pressure from regulators and investors to separate these two businesses. Regulators are concerned that investors do not fully understand the built-in conflicts or the related economic arrangements between affiliates. Disclosure does not solve the problem, and investors are leery about advisors pushing house-made products.

In 2016, Wells Fargo employees created millions of fraudulent bank and credit card accounts, ultimately leading to hefty fines and the firing of several key executives, including the CEO. As regulators investigated the situation, they found that millions of investors had suffered from the bank's aggressive cross-selling practices. Beginning in 2018, the bank and wealth management units were fined or required to refund billions of dollars, including a $1 billion penalty for mortgage-related issues in April, $480 million for fake accounts in May, $114 million for wealth management clients in June, $505 million for forex in July, and $2.1 billion for toxic sales practices in August. In addition to the fines and refunds, the firm has suffered irreparable reputation damage.

The Wells Fargo scandal, and other abuses exposed after the global financial crisis, cast a spotlight on conflicts across business lines, from banking and wealth management to research and investment banking. HNW investors have become much more aware of these issues and concerned about whether an advisor is really working in their best interests.

I predict that a large bank will separate its businesses and eliminate these potential conflicts of interest. If one bank splits its businesses into discrete organizations, others will likely follow suit, especially if a split-off business demonstrates the ability to grow.

Education as a Differentiator

In a crowded marketplace where investors have a difficult time differentiating among the firms, wealth advisors often need to lead with education. Internal and external credentialing will become increasingly important for advisors to improve their knowledge and distinguish them from the pack. Specialized advanced training will be at a premium. A big part of a wealth advisor's value proposition will be in imparting knowledge around complex investments, product evolution, and non-investment-related issues such as trust and estate planning, charitable giving, and dealing with concentrated positions.

Educational organizations like the Investments & Wealth Institute, the CAIA Association, the Financial Planning Association, and the CFA Institute must continue to evolve their training curriculum to address the changing landscape. The curriculum must be appropriate for wealth advisors and the clients they serve, addressing their specific needs and incorporating a changing array of investment strategies. These organizations will need to recognize the investment and noninvestment challenges facing wealth advisors, and offer continuing education, white papers, and materials to help advisors continue to hone their craft.

Scale and Efficiency Are at a Premium

The wealth management industry will continue to face fee compression, and successful firms will need to seek scale and efficiency to survive the next 10 years. Squeezed margins mean that wealth management firms will need to change their coverage models, with smaller accounts migrating to automated advice solutions and advisor teams serving larger, more complex relationships. Advisors emphasize capturing a larger slice of the wealth pie to augment falling fees.

Wealth advisors and their offices are the biggest cost components, so firms will disintermediate advisors wherever possible, jettisoning smaller accounts to a service center model. They will cut operations and administrative support to rein in costs and will leverage technology to replace human interactions where they can.

Of course, the trade-off may involve losing wealth advisors to an RIA model and disenfranchising investors who migrate to the lowest-cost solution. This will be a difficult balancing act to grow the client base and shrink their cost structure, without losing what they need to retain. The search for efficiency has been underway for the past several years. Some firms will be able to take market share; others may be consolidated into another firm.

Commissions Will Be Free

Commissions have been falling dramatically over the past couple of decades, and Schwab and Fidelity have already announced commission-free trading. In reality, those firms were already less dependent on commissions. They were trying to gain market share from wirehouses, which had moved away from commissions as their sole revenue source decades earlier. Trading will inevitably become commission free across the industry in the not too distant future. As with free ETFs, this will simply mean that the firm is capturing revenues elsewhere. Schwab and Fidelity gave away trading commissions in an attempt to open more accounts and generate more revenue from cash sitting idly in money market funds.

With large pools of low-yielding assets, Schwab and Fidelity are competing on scale. But these firms make money in ways that may not be apparent to most investors, including receiving payment for order flow, making money by lending securities, using affiliated products in model portfolios, and creating revenue-sharing relationships with asset managers. Charles Schwab founded his firm to disrupt the status quo of fixed commission pricing. The company has led the way in dropping prices as a way of gaining market share from the do-it-yourself crowd. Over the years, this has become a smaller and smaller portion of the firm's overall revenue stream.

These large firms do not arbitrarily give things away. They can shift their economic model to give up revenue in one business unit and recoup it in another way. There's nothing wrong with this per se—but investors need to understand that "free isn't always free."

Artificial Intelligence

Wealth management firms have been searching for this holy grail for years, trying to understand what clients want and need before clients know it themselves. This could help advisors know the best strategy for a client, cross-sell products, and anticipate a client's decision to switch firms. Can these firms use artificial intelligence to learn more about a client's needs? Can they teach computers how to identify client behaviors?

Wealth management firms are investing in technology to solve these problems and gain an edge on their competitors. They have made progress with risk-profile questionnaires, propensity models, and trend analysis, but they are still searching for computers that can teach themselves. In the next decade, artificial intelligence will probably help wealth management firms maximize client relationships and solve complex problems with a single keystroke. Artificial intelligence will help advisors anticipate client needs, provide better outcomes, and deepen client relationships. However, artificial intelligence probably can't replace a good wealth advisor or help investors weather market volatility. AI lacks empathy and has no ability to read nonverbal cues.

NAVIGATING THE CHANGING LANDSCAPE

Wealth advisors will need to anticipate changes and adapt their practices to respond to the ever-changing wealth management landscape. Those who resist these sweeping changes will likely be left behind, and those who embrace change will likely flourish. Whether or not all my predictions come true, it is safe to assume that there will be dramatic changes in the wealth advisor's value proposition and the way they serve their clients. Successful advisors will embrace technology as a tool, and not fear it as a threat to their value proposition.

Wealth advisory practices will need to adopt a team-oriented model and become younger and more diverse to relate to the investors they serve. They'll need more women, millennials, and minorities. These teams will need to possess a broader set of capabilities, evolving beyond merely providing portfolio-level advice and *right-sizing* their practices to serve their clients well. Wealth advisors will need to embrace a goals-based investing process to solve for a family's various needs simultaneously.

Wealth advisors will need to hone their investment acumen and expand their toolbox to include alternative investments (private markets and hedge funds) and sustainable investing, and they will need to educate their clients regarding the role and use of the strategies and the structural trade-offs. As wealth advisors continue to evolve their practices, they will likely consider multiple business models (wirehouses, aggregators, RIAs, etc.) and must determine which model best aligns with their practice and clients' interest. These advisors will need to invest in themselves and continue their journey of enlightenment, participating in advanced educational programs that help them meet their clients' goals.

Wealth advisors may need to evolve their practices and economic model to better align with their value proposition. Asset-based fees are preferable to commissions, but advisor compensation is tied to the portfolio, a fact that ignores the vast array of services that an advisor provides. Subscription models, project-oriented pricing, retainer fees, and hourly fees may evolve as preferable future models. Like everything else in our industry, investors will affect the way fees are paid and the fee level that makes sense for all parties.

HNW AND UHNW INVESTORS

HNW and UHNW investors will likely benefit from an expanding menu of investing options, in the number and quality of products. The first generation of alternative investments was built for large institutions and family offices. Consequently, these products had high minimums, limited liquidity, and long time horizons. In recent years, private capital firms and hedge funds have recognized the demand from HNW investors and have introduced high-quality products in more innovative structures.

In the future, HNW investors will be able to evaluate wealth advisors based on service, price, and investment capabilities, in an app like Yelp, Trip Advisor, or Open Table. They will benefit from more advisors moving to an independent fiduciary model and more scrutiny regarding potential conflicts of interest. HNW investors can choose to engage a wealth advisor for all or part of their wealth management needs and can easily access and integrate other experts through a more tech-efficient platform.

KEY TAKEAWAYS

I began this book by reviewing the evolution and changing value proposition of wealth advisors. I have challenged advisors to solve for the needs and objectives of HNW investors and expand their capabilities beyond managing a client's portfolio to include a deeper understanding of trust and estate issues, tax management techniques, and dealing with concentrated positions.

Wealth management firms and asset managers have also responded to the changing landscape, adjusting their economic and service models, while still competing for market share. Product evolution has helped usher in a vast array of new strategies, including sustainability, factor investing, private equity, private credit, real assets, equity hedge, event driven, relative value, macro, and multi-strategy, in a variety of structures that include ETFs, feeder funds, tender-offer funds, and interval funds. Wealth advisors now have an expanded toolbox, but they need more education to use these tools wisely.

I examined the limitations of traditional finance, including MPT, and discussed behavioral finance and the inherent biases that we all exhibit (including advisors). MPT assumes that investors are rational and will select optimal portfolios; it assumes that the future will be like the past. Not all investors seek to maximize returns or minimize risk. Most investors are solving for multiple goals with different time frames to achieve those goals. Throughout the book, I made the case for goals-based investing as a more appropriate way of solving for client needs, marrying attributes of MPT and behavioral finance.

I discussed the challenges of using stale capital market assumptions, where investors risk falling short of their expected return and income targets. Yesterday's playbook will likely fail to achieve a client's goals and objectives in the future, based on substantially lower capital market assumptions for traditional investments, generational low bond yields, and increasing correlations across asset classes. Alternative investments can help address the lower return environment, offer alternative sources of income, and provide broader diversification than traditional investments alone.

To help bring some of these concepts to life, I shared some of my personal experiences working with UHNW families, emphasizing how to engage them—and how they viewed and valued their advisors. Although UHNW families have more complex financial needs than most of us, their concerns about family and values remain an integral part of the relationship. Rather than being overwhelmed by a family's wealth, advisors must instead focus on solving their needs in the most transparent way possible, engaging other trusted advisors in a coordinated fashion.

I hope that my book has encouraged wealth advisors to continue their *lifetime of learning* and my insights and experience have helped in thinking about this ever-evolving industry. I also hope that my book has offered insights to family offices and HNW investors who access unbundled advice, leveraging multiple experts to achieve their objectives.

In this final chapter, I imagined what the industry will look like in the next 10 years and made predictions about some possible transformational changes. Some of these changes may be easier for advisors than others—and some advisors have already begun this transformation. Issues like greater diversity in advisory practices may be harder to attain over the short run, but will be essential for future growth. No matter which of my predictions come true, I am confident that the wealth management industry will change a great deal over the next decade. To succeed, wealth advisors must anticipate and respond to these changes. Successful wealth advisors will embrace this changing landscape and flourish by adapting their value proposition and the way they serve investors.

Notes

CHAPTER 1

1. Boghai, Pooneh, Olivia Howard, Lakshmi Prakash, and Jill Zucker, "Women Are the Next Wave of Growth in U.S. Wealth Management," July 29, 2020, https://www.mckinsey.com/industries/financial-services/our-insights/women -as-the-next-wave-of-growth-in-us-wealth-management.

CHAPTER 2

1. "Capgemini 2020 World Wealth Report," July 2020, https://www.capgemini .com/us-en/news/research-world-wealth-report-2020/.
2. Beyer, Charlotte, "Relationship Alpha: The Emerging Competitive Advantage in Wealth Management," CFA Institute Research Foundation, 2019, https:// www.cfainstitute.org/-/media/documents/article/rf-brief/relationship-alpha .ashx.
3. "Capgemini 2020 World Wealth Report," July 2020, https://www.capgemini .com/us-en/news/research-world-wealth-report-2020/.
4. Brunel, Jean, *Goals-Based Wealth Management: An Integrated and Practical Approach to Changing the Structure of Wealth Advisory Practices*, Hoboken, NJ: Wiley, 2015.

CHAPTER 3

1. Cerulli Associates, "Mitigating the Impact of Behavioral Biases," July 2019, https://investmentsandwealth.org/getmedia/dea8bde8-2399-4534-b97f -541dd7e46123/Cerulli-whitepaper-Mitigating-the-Impact-of-Advisors -Behavioral-Biases-002.pdf.
2. Liu, Berlinda, and Gaurav Sinha, "SPIVA U.S. Mid-Year Scorecard," October 2020, https://www.spglobal.com/spdji/en/documents/spiva/spiva-us-year-end -2020.pdf.
3. Littlechild, Julie, "2020 Investor Research Canada: The Current Crisis, the Impact of Client Loyalty, and the Implications for Your Business," July 15, 2020, https://investmentsandwealth.org/getmedia/ff1dbeac-749c-4aac-87e5-b0f7e 8ee7dc0/Toews-Special-Report-FINAL-6-3-2020.pdf.

4. Kinniry, Francis, Colleen Jaconetti, and Michael DiJoseph, "Putting a Value on Advisors Value: Quantifying Vanguard Advisor's Alpha," Vanguard Research, February 2019, https://www.vanguard.com/pdf/ISGQVAA.pdf.

5. Shefrin, Hersh, and Meir Statman, "Behavioral Portfolio Theory," *Journal of Financial and Quantitative Analysis*, June 2000, http://efinance.org.cn/cn/fm/Behavioral%20Portfolio%20Theory.pdf.

6. Statman, Meir, "Portfolios for Normal People," *Investments & Wealth Monitor*, January-February 2017, https://investmentsandwealth.org/getattachment/Investors/Investor-Resources/Articles/IWM17MayJun-FinanceForNormalPeople.pdf?lang=en-US.

CHAPTER 5

1. Liu, Berlinda, and Gaurav Sinha, "SPIVA Mid-Year 2020 Scorecard," September 2020, https://www.spglobal.com/spdji/en/documents/spiva/spiva-us-year-end-2020.pdf.

2. Investment Company Institute, "ICI Fact Book, 2020," https://www.ici.org/system/files/attachments/pdf/2020_factbook.pdf.

3. Davidow, Anthony, "Strategic Beta Strategies: Do They Work Outside Our Borders," *Investments & Wealth Monitor*, November-December 2018.

4. Davidow, Anthony, "Strategic Beta Strategies: Evaluating Different Approaches," *Investments & Wealth Monitor,* September-October 2016.

5. Davidow, Anthony, "Strategic Beta Strategies: Do They Work Outside Our Borders," *Investments & Wealth Monitor*, November-December 2018.

CHAPTER 7

1. Yale News, "Investment Return of 6.8% Brings Yale Endowment Value to $31.2 Billion," September 24, 2020, https://news.yale.edu/2020/09/24/investment-return-68-brings-yale-endowment-value-312-billion

2. Buffet, Warren, and Jamie Dimon, "Short-Termism Is Harming the Economy," *Wall Street Journal*, June 6, 2018.

3. McKinsey & Company, *A New Decade for Private Markets*, February 2020, https://www.mckinsey.com/~/media/mckinsey/industries/private%20equity%20and%20principal%20investors/our%20insights/mckinseys%20private%20markets%20annual%20review/mckinsey-global-private-markets-review-2020-v4.ashx.

4. Preqin, "2020 Preqin Global Private Debt Report," February 2020, https://www.preqin.com/insights/global-reports/2021-preqin-global-private-debt-report.

5. Davidow, Anthony, "Private Equity: Innovation and Evolution," *Investments & Wealth Monitor*, November-December 2019.

CHAPTER 8

1. Fink, Larry, "A Fundamental Reshaping of Finance," BlackRock, 2020.
2. Stevens, Pippa, "Nasdaq Proposal Would Require Greater Diversity on Company Boards," CNBC, December 1, 2020.
3. The Forum for Sustainable and Responsible Investing, "The US SIF Foundation's 2020 Biennial *Report on US Sustainable and Impact Investing Trends*," November 16, 2020, https://www.ussif.org/trends.
4. Cook, Jackie, and Tom Lauricella, "How Big Fund Families Voted on Climate Change: 2020 Edition," Morningstar, September 28, 2020.
5. New York Life, "Dispelling the Five Common Myths," November 2019.
6. Baghai, Pooneh, Olivia Howard, Lakshmi Prakash, and Jill Zucker, "Women as the Next Wave of Growth in Wealth Management," McKinsey & Company, July 29, 2020, https://www.mckinsey.com/industries/financial-services/our-insights/women-as-the-next-wave-of-growth-in-us-wealth-management.
7. Hale, Jon, "Sustainable Funds Weather the First Quarter Better Than Conventional Funds," Morningstar, April 3, 2020.
8. Riding, Siobhan, "Majority of ESG Funds Outperform Wider Market over 10 Years," *Financial Times*, June 13, 2020.
9. Guido Giese, Zoltan Nagy, and Linda-Eling Lee, "Deconstructing ESG Ratings Performance," MSCI ESG Research LLC, June 2020.
10. Guido Giese, Zoltan Nagy, and Linda-Eling Lee, "Deconstructing ESG Ratings Performance," MSCI ESG Research LLC, June 2020.
11. Baker, Sophie, "Global ESG-Data Driven Assets Hit $40.5 Trillion," *Pensions and Investments,* July 2020.

CHAPTER 9

1. Chhabra, Ashvin, "Beyond Markowitz: A Comprehensive Wealth Allocation Framework for Individual Investors," *Journal of Wealth Management*, Spring 2005, https://jwm.pm-research.com/content/7/4/8.
2. Brunel, Jean, *Goals-Based Wealth Management: An Integrated and Practical Approach to Changing the Structure of Wealth Advisory Practices*, Hoboken, NJ: Wiley, 2015.

CHAPTER 10

1. McKinsey & Company, "On the Cusp of Change: North American Wealth Management in 2030," January 2020, https://www.mckinsey.com/industries/financial-services/our-insights/banking-matters/on-the-cusp-of-change-north-american-wealth-management-in-2030.

Index

Page references followed by an *f* or *t* refer to figures and tables, respectively.

About the Author

Tony Davidow, CIMA, is president of T. Davidow Consulting, an independent advisory firm focused on the needs and challenges facing the financial services industry. Davidow leverages his diverse experiences to deliver research and analysis to sophisticated advisors, asset managers, and wealthy families. He has held senior leadership roles at Morgan Stanley, Charles Schwab, Guggenheim Investments, and Kidder Peabody among others. He is focused on developing and delivering content relating to advanced asset allocation strategies, alternative investments, factor investing, sustainable investing, and other topics. In 2020, Davidow was recognized by the Investments and Wealth Institute, with the prestigious Wealth Management Impact Award, which honors individuals who have contributed exceptional advancements in the field of private wealth management.